I0488053

RECOVERING THE SPIRIT OF MANAGEMENT

RECOVERING THE SPIRIT OF MANAGEMENT

A Reader-Interactive Experience of Self Discovery

IZZY S. JUSTICE

Authors Choice Press

San Jose New York Lincoln Shanghai

Recovering the Spirit of Management
A Reader-Interactive Experience of Self Discovery

All Rights Reserved © 2001 by Izzy Syed Justice

No part of this book may be reproduced or transmitted in any form or by any means, graphic, electronic, or mechanical, including photocopying, recording, taping, or by any information storage or retrieval system, without the permission in writing from the publisher.

Authors Choice Press
an imprint of iUniverse.com, Inc.

For information address:
iUniverse.com, Inc.
5220 S 16th, Ste. 200
Lincoln, NE 68512
www.iuniverse.com

ISBN: 0-595-17664-X

Printed in the United States of America

This Book and Journal Belongs To:

_____

Date of Journal Entries

_____

Dedication

How could I have imagined the great humility, serenity, and joy that comes from being loved by one's soul mate? For my dear wife, Stephanie.

Acknowledgements

Gary Mason—my eternal mentor whose life and death continue to inspire and humble me daily. I write to honor you and what you have taught me.

Terry Cowles, Andy Garber, and Rick Smith—three of the finest men I have ever worked with. I will not forget the generosity of your wisdom. Rick Smith and his passion are the true inspiration of this book.

A special "thanks" to Tom Doorley for taking me under his wing and coaching me through the process of creating and publishing this book. And to John Bonno and Diann Lynch—thanks for opening your lives to me.

Additional thanks to Marcy Fantel, Melissa Freshman, Debbie Fox, Meridith Rentz and Kim Vogel for all their insights and diligent work as editors, co-writers and friends.

Foreword

By:
Thomas L. Doorley,III
Author of Value-Creating Growth

Without a doubt, great, high performing organizations, are blessed with great leaders. Clearly, effective leadership is a common underpinning of success. Yet, in the nearly thirty years during which I've counseled such leaders I've never ceased to be impressed by the importance of the next level, people called "managers". Without talented, committed teams to execute core strategies, to motivate the broad reach of the enterprise, to care for the development of the young, no organization will survive, let alone thrive. For the first time, in a long time, this issue is being addressed, here, now, by Izzy Justice.

The time is right for a focus on the spirit, soul, and heart of management. The "New Economy" that is lifting the developed nations so strongly is based on productivity and growth. Productivity arrived first. After two decades of slow productivity performance, we are in the midst of a resurgence. Annual productivity gains in the west are double the rates achieved from the early 1970s through the mid 1990s. The leverage of information and its technology provide much of the lift. But critically, management has learned to shoulder a continual and increasing burden of this drive for performance. Possibly, at the outset of the productivity surge, management was in fact underutilized. But anyone who has spent a week or even a day with these folks recently would be daunted by the pressure on them.

Unfortunately, and oddly, little attention has been directed to these individuals. If we are to maintain or, as is our collective hope, enhance further our productivity levels, we have to address this issue. The managers among us need more care, feeding, training and honor, than they have received recently. Izzy Justice does so.

Think of your own model of a great organization. Ask how it remains successful. My guess is it will be blessed by a self perpetuating cadre of extremely effective managers. At this writing almost all of us would agree that General Electric, GE, would rank as a highly successful enterprise. In fact GE may be the most responsive large scale, peacetime, private sector organization, ever. GE is well known for the quality for its leaders, not least of which is its current Chairman, Jack Welch. But look inside its sustained performance and you'll see an enormous effort dedicated to the continual development of its cadre of managers. I have taught the Business Management Course with GE staff and can testify to the amount and quality of effort expended to assure that the great future leaders will keep coming, and that the managers will keep to their task in the heart, and depths of the structure. Rather than overworking the popular attention on the top the message we should take from GE is the work done to ensure the middle.

In my experience I've found the best teachers to be those who have the best experience at the challenge at hand. Izzy Justice qualifies. Not only is he by his nature a teacher, he is today a manager as well. His life's work is as a manager. The people you will read about are drawn from reality. Thus the counsel given, and the process defined, stand the test. I am impressed with the touch and feel of this work. I am hopeful that it can lead the way to a more profound understanding of how to liberate the talent embedded in all of our enterprises. To paraphrase, talent is a terrible thing to waste. If we hope to win the rewards the New Economy promises, and potentially promises us all, we must find the means to give hope, counsel and meaning to those we call managers.

Join in, now, in a journey. Learn from it. Apply it, to your own career, or to those you mentor. How we develop our managers will determine how we will win as enterprises, as economies, as society. They are the engines of today's performance. They are our future.

From the author...

For many years now my job has been to help an organization achieve its optimal performance by building bridges between leadership groups and employees, and by installing processes and enabling technologies that encourage the desired behaviors. I get asked by clients to anticipate and dissipate potential show-stoppers ("people issues") during major transitions—be it a merger or an acquisition, a major systems implementation, a new global strategy, or during significant internal change such as downsizing or changes in leadership. As the Change Management Consultant for many organizations going through these types of organizational stress, I coach all levels of an organization and help shift paradigms of management. I hear the troublesome stories from all sides and offer remedial action. As a manager myself, I work most closely with the middle tier of management. As a consultant, however, I become privy to information and stories that my peers in the client organization are not. It is these coalesced stories that I bring to this book. They are real life experiences of many managers—and I trust that in their stories you will see yourself and learn from the solutions to challenges they face. In the myriad of issues faced, I hope you will find the thread of humanity that weaves through all of us—especially managers.

My personal life spans the globe, and during this journey I have committed myself to making sense of the untenable chaos that comes from being more and more aware of the complexity of the human being—and all the inter-woven roles required of him to survive and be content in today's equally complex world. I am a man, a husband, an uncle, a son, a brother, a nephew, a consultant, a leader, a follower, a coach, an employee, a peer, a writer, a tax-payer, a customer, a salesman and much more. Each role dictates a different set of behaviors, information, and skills. I hope you will discover all your roles, how they impact one another and your overall well being.

Preface

I am writing a story about the heart and the spirit. I concede that this is not a novel concept. Matters of the heart and soul have been topics of debate, great artistry, passionate speeches, and systemic coercion since the advent of time itself. Indeed, I must further concede that the soaring wealth of knowledge of the average person today would dramatically overshadow that of geniuses of centuries past. So, why do I dare write the same story? More importantly, why should you, the reader, with the almost euphoric abundance of knowledge to which you have ready access, waste your valuable time muddling through my story and the exercises in it?

I was once told that the world would never be rid of pain so long as one was raised in a family, tried to love something or someone, had to work with another person, or tried to *change* something or someone for the better. I would contend that the human being has not evolved into a more complex creature through the centuries, but, instead, has become more aware of the complexities within him.

Do you understand how complex you are? Do you know what compels you? Do you know what distresses you and why? Do you know what you love and hate and why? Do you know why you do even half the things you do? Do you know why you seek the things you seek? Do you know what success means to you?…I mean, do you really know? And what about the answers to these same questions for your family members or significant others? Your best friend—your boss—your coworkers? Do you know what makes them tick? Balancing this delicate and changing complexity can be exhausting.

Why bother?

My first truth is that you must bother. You will not survive very long as a social creature in the world today without bothering to understand. You will have to demonstrate fitness in a vast array of challenges.

Our complexity could partly be attributed to the cumulative effect of using others as mirrors or benchmarks for ourselves. As these relationships/people have become more complex, so too have we. The *pace* of evolution has accelerated dramatically. The stimuli that incessantly bombard our lives (experiences, TV, film, Internet, books, music, people) have forced more and more of us to compartmentalize—store our experiences in conveniently organized mental filing cabinets. These experiences often stay there, unresolved, for a long time. When they are finally revealed, it is usually in times of great despair, and because of this, usually muck things up. If there existed a hierarchy of these archived memories, one would find only about two or three trend-setting ones at the bottom—which shoulder the other ones at the root of our personality tree.

My second truth is that these 'anchor' experiences are our character-defining experiences. They define (in the sense of cause and effect) the behavior we exhibit. The result? We subconsciously surround ourselves with reinforcing behaviors and experiences—we seek what comforts us. Although engaging in what comforts us will, in most cases, lead to some perceived operating mode of success, especially as defined by others, it is rarely in this mode where the real joy of life resides. It is certainly not in this mode where harmony between you, as known by the world, and you, as known by only you, is reached. And your performance under the bright lights of your inner stage is very often melancholic.

So why should you read this book? Because you must take time to bother. Carl Jung once wrote, "Meaning makes a great many things endurable—perhaps everything."

You must make time to understand how you are complex and figure out why you are complex. You must realize that when you go to work you take *all* that complexity with you—and so does everyone else.

The time to pretend that we are robots—capable of everyday Oscar-worthy performances on the world stage of work under the guise of 'Professionalism' is over. Going home to yourself, to your significant other and to your families and pretending that you can leave work at work is no longer practical or even necessary. Make no mistake—you take *all* that complexity home, too. You cannot pretend or hide anymore. People know. We're getting smarter. And is it not emotionally exhausting?

An epidemic quest to learn to accept ourselves, to learn to prosper at things we truly love and to be a star on both stages, is well underway. All over the country people are saying: I just want to be happy. I want to enjoy what I do. It is no longer all about money. I think I deserve better. I think I can do more. **My life ought to mean more.**

This book presents a model to help you understand your complexity. It will challenge you and stretch you out of your comfort zone. It will allow you to process those experiences in your life that define you and help you understand how others are defined. You will find that this understanding is what I call a "leverage understanding"—understand this and you will understand all of you. Understand the root causes of your being and you will understand all the symptoms. We do well at understanding only the symptoms and mitigating them with a cure for the day, for the week, for the experience—but we fall disturbingly short of a holistic cure for our lives.

Diana Trilling wrote just before her death, "Where do our thoughts go when we are growing up and suppose that we have no further use for them?"

The story in this book is a unique one; it is the fictional journey of three managers in the American workforce. It begins in Chapter Two, in January, 1999, and ends exactly a year later in December, 1999. **As a reader, you will be invited to follow the personal and professional lives of these three characters and wrestle with the challenges each faces during the course of the year in their respective lives.** These challenges are not exclusive to management—but are prevalent within this demographic in the workforce today. So whether you are just out of college or have 20 or more years vested in your profession, understanding the layer of people between you should be an equally enlightening and educational exercise.

You are also invited to play a unique part in this story—to join in! Yes—participate in their lives, share their challenges, joy, pain, and help create your own "memoir" for your personal and professional life. Interspersed in the story are carefully sequenced questions (*under a different font*) and space for you to write your responses. The 'reader-interaction' format is different and will cause you to reflect in a unique way. As a rule, you should complete each exercise prior to proceeding to the next one. So you will need a pen or pencil to 'do' the book. Engaging an audience in the activity of learning enhances both the assimilation and retention of knowledge; by being engaged in the story, I hope this book will become 'an experience' and not just 'a read.'

The reader-interactive exercises for you in the story will be similar to those that the three characters are facing—so you will have a companion. It is very much like going to a gym and working out with someone, as opposed to working out by yourself or, worse yet, just watching someone else work out. To continue with this metaphor, if you worked out with a personal trainer, he or she would carefully navigate you through a series of exercises congruent with what your physical goals and limitations are. That is the model for the exercises in this book.

Practice makes perfect—so use the exercises in this book as 'simulations' of what life may surprise you with. You will be better prepared for the unpredictable challenges of life by having thought through the various scenarios.

Because this is a book, your information is confidential. It might be interesting to 'do' the book with trustworthy companions in your personal or professional circle of friends and compare answers. Have a workshop or a dinner with friends and discuss your responses. Here, the value might not be just in what I write and postulate or even in what you write—but in the conversations and the intellectual friction that will undoubtedly result.

At the end of the book, you should have two books and two stories—my story and your story. Use it as a memoir—give it to your significant other or save it for your children.

Finally, know that the fictional story is written by a manager (me) primarily for managers and about managers. The three characters, Alex Montana, Briana Jones and Gabriel Sloan, though fictional, are based on real people. All three live in different parts of the country and are pursuing different vocations. As stated earlier, their journey begins when they all meet at a unique leadership workshop in Atlanta, Georgia, and are coincidentally grouped to support each other during the course of the year. The follow-up workshop is scheduled in Miami in early December, where the three are to collectively report on what they have learned from and taught each other. The facilitator of the workshop, Iseus Tanga, is an immigrant whose profound wisdom quickly becomes the source of great inspiration and friendship for all three.

I hope reading and working through this book will be as challenging and rewarding of an experience for you as it has been for me. **I hope you will embrace this book as an opportunity to introduce yourself to you—** and to welcome the learning as an experience that ultimately only you will benefit from. The exercises will challenge you and take some time, but, again, documenting your learning will greatly enhance your experience. Good luck with meeting the stranger in you!

Chapter One

Chapter One

WHY FOCUS ON MANAGEMENT?

A Room with a View

Two men, both seriously ill, occupied the same hospital room. One man was allowed to sit up in his bed for an hour each afternoon to help drain the fluid from his lungs. His bed was next to the room's only window.

The other man had to spend all his time flat on his back. The men talked for hours on end. They spoke of their wives and families, their homes, their jobs, their involvement in the military service, and where they had been on vacation. And every afternoon when the man in the bed by the window could sit up, he would pass the time by describing to his room-mate all the things he could see outside the window. The man in the other bed began to live for those one-hour periods where his world would be broadened and enlivened by all the activity and color of the world outside. The window overlooked a park with a lovely lake. Ducks and swans played on the water while children sailed their model boats. Young lovers walked arm in arm amidst flowers of every color of the rainbow. Grand old trees graced the landscape, and a fine view of the city skyline could be seen in the distance.

As the man by the window described all this in exquisite detail, the man on the other side of the room would close his eyes and imagine the pictur-esque scene. One warm afternoon the man by the window described a parade passing by. Although the other man couldn't hear the band—he could see it in his mind's eye as the gentleman by the window portrayed it with descriptive words.

Days and weeks passed. One morning, the day nurse arrived to bring water for their baths, only to find the lifeless body of the man by the window, *who had died peacefully in his sleep. She was saddened and called the hospital attendants to take the body away. As soon as it seemed appropriate, the other man asked if he could be moved next to the window. The nurse was happy to make the switch, and after making sure he was comfortable, she left him alone. Slowly, painfully, he propped himself up on one elbow to take his first look at the world outside. Finally, he would have the joy of seeing it for himself.*

He strained to slowly turn to look out the window beside the bed. It faced a blank wall. The man asked the nurse what could have compelled his deceased roommate who had described such wonderful things outside this window.

The nurse responded that the man was blind and could not even see the wall. She said, "Perhaps he just wanted to encourage you."

Author Unknown
Source: Internet

So why focus on management? I have found that the vast majority of books and guiding thought on management and leadership are written not by managers, but by thought leaders, the management gurus. They are typically written for the 'executive leadership' of an organization and not for managers. The executive audience, goes the thought, is that echelon of the organizational chart with the authority and power to make strategic decisions impacting all levels within an organization. Now, let's be honest—what percentage of the workforce falls into this demographic? That's right—a very small one. Typically, less than 5% of an organization possesses this kind of authority and power.

I am not discounting the perspectives of these management gurus, nor discarding the vignettes they can share with their consortium of successful followers, but their primary audience is not management and their constant barrage of assumptions that we, managers, have control over company policies, total control of our careers and total control of our destinies are arguable and troublesome. **Not everyone can be a Jack Welch or a Michael Dell. Not everyone has the responsibility of being at the helm of a company-wide vision and the power to materialize it.** There are undoubtedly exceptions—but most of us simply are not molded from this rock. The few that are are often caged by age-old bureaucracy, hijacked by traditional stereotypes associated with being 'young' managers, and have limited access to the information they need to make better, faster, and strategic decisions. A great deal has been written about harnessing this collective 'brain power' of an organization—but little from the perspective of management. Yet all would agree that it is this group that is traditionally responsible for 'making things happen.' It is management that is charged with the less glamorous 'in-the-trenches' responsibilities.

Internal HR surveys of many companies reveal a troubling truth—the most content segments of an organization are its new employees (shorter tenure) or its senior executives (longer tenure). The dreadful dip in employee satisfaction bottoms out with managers. What is troubling this group? Why is it always managers? Why are they unhappy?

Further consider that most of the counsel dispensed these days is institutional or systemic—not individualistic and intrinsic. A well-designed organizational framework with integrated performance management matrices for optimal productivity is certainly needed. However, this type of strategic responsibility is traditionally given to the executive leadership to envision, and for the HR department (or a consultant) to develop and implement. How does the life of a manager fit into all this? How can a manager find reward and fulfillment in what he/she is held accountable for? **How can we motivate ourselves to make the most out of this intensely frustrating position in our careers while we wait for our superiors to either promote us or remove the barriers they consider arcane and unknowingly sustain?** What are the implications of waiting? Are our values inferior just because they are different from those in power? How much compromise is too much?

WHO IS MANAGEMENT?

Management is traditionally defined as the second or third tier (of about six or seven levels) of management in an organization. Some defining characteristics of this group are:

- Aged between 28-40 with an average of 10 years of professional experience
- Typically responsible for 'doing the work' (most of the workday is spent on hands-on tasks and activities that produce the output that is desired and sold by the company)
- Often chartered with leading company project teams or play leadership roles for a younger (new graduates) or less experienced workforce, leading departments, projects, initiatives, or small or segmented groups of employees
- Often consulted with on major decisions by senior management but not responsible for the decisions

What makes this demographic unique?

Historically, every manager is in a state of transition or a change. This group experiences many 'firsts' as it plays out time, fate and circumstance. The newness of the many challenges in personal and professional endeavors makes for an emotionally and intellectually challenging phase in one's career and life. Some of the challenges that come to the forefront are:

1. Money

By this time in the career of a manager, most debts (like college loans) are paid off and investment planning of some sort has begun. **This is the first time this group has had any disposable income worth writing home about.** The new wave of financial freedom is a sparkling experience. Some managers who take home well above six figures even feel guilty about their financial success and are not entirely comfortable pampering themselves. Much of management is making significantly more money today than their parents did at this stage in their careers.

2.   Lifestyles

Managers are relatively new at being married, having children or owning a home. These new experiences are often accompanied by a sudden onset of new demands that can be exhausting. **Marriage and having children are the types of experiences that people, no matter how much they have observed or read about the subjects, are ever quite prepared enough for.** The learning curve is both exciting and challenging.

3.   Ideas

The hallmark of this group could be in the abundance of ideas it has on how to make things better—at work, in the communities they live in and in the world. What this group offers in desire, it lacks in competence; what it offers in energy and optimism, it lacks in influence. **Resistance Creep** (the notion of a great idea dying because of inadequate sponsorship from the right people) leads to despondent behavior and a pessimistic view of one's ability to truly drive needed change. Coping with the resulting despair causes frustration, and managers either wait and eventually age through this stage or find employment elsewhere. The new job often results in the same challenges—but with a little more cash to take home.

4.   Self Esteem

This is the rising tide of one's life when one begins to feel quite comfortable with what one does not know. One has spent one's entire life being taught and absorbing information and knowledge and the modus operandi seem to be changing. The manager becomes conversant and competent in adding value. But it is not enough to know what one knows; one must also know what one does not know as well as where to obtain this missing knowledge. **The ability to orchestrate a series of activities that leads to a desired output becomes the new sought-after competency.** No longer is technical competence the paramount performance measure for the manager's success. This self affirmation by the manager often leads to heightened self esteem. **The vast unknown has shrunk.** They have figured out how the world operates and how to be successful in it despite its ambiguity and uncertainty.

5. Heroes

The people that managers once revered have now become human, mortal, and with flaws. Parents of managers suddenly appear much smarter to managers than they ever gave them credit for. Amazingly enough, managers are now role models for a younger generation—whether that is at work, at home, or in the communities they live in. This new status can be an overwhelming and humbling experience. Moreover, managers find great optimism in finding mentors after whom to model their lives.

6. The Manager Family

If married, both spouses are typically working. Whether married or single, a manager is more often than not removed from his/her social and family network and support system. **The lucrative offers of work often come with this seemingly small price: relocation.** The impact of not having either the traditional family support structure or one made of up old and genuine friends can be unpredictably devastating.

7. Single

The generation of managers today has more singles than any other generation. An overwhelming number of managers have either never been married or are divorced. In the closed system of human existence, this fact and its implications on the American workforce, both positive and negative, cannot be ignored.

8. Skills

The skill sets required by managers today are dramatically different from those required by management of a generation ago. The technological evolution has dictated a myriad of competencies—the most common of which is to be willing to change constantly and lead by championing those changes. The unlimited variety in jobs today is also astounding in comparison to generations past. There are jobs today, great, challenging, and rewarding jobs that were not even conceivable as recently as 15 years ago. Virtual environments and teams are the norm today. **The manager has borne the brunt of both the benefits and challenges of this dynamic job market.**

9. Diversity

The diversity of the workforce is dramatically different from that of a generation ago. The workforce today comprises a myriad of religious and spiritual workers. More women, more minorities of all backgrounds, and a phenomenal spectrum of styles and personalities today make the manager's job more challenging than ever. **Remember, it is the manager who** has the most direct contact and responsibility for the en masse work-force of any organization. Not enough emphasis to this dimension of management is given and it might be the most important skill set for the manager of tomorrow.

   10.   Value System

The value system of managers today is different from generations past and comparable to the difference in values between Generation X and Baby Boomers. **Managers want and demand employers that honor their values to the community, to diversity, to work-life balance, and to equal opportunity.** This group necessitates its values to match the values of the companies it works for, and there is very little force-fitting of values as in generations past.

In summary, management is a unique group of people with a dynamic set of challenges that warrants attention. The type of limited expert counsel that this group has traditionally received needs to be changed because the group has grown and society and the world at large have evolved and created new challenges.

"There are two kinds of tragedies in life: one is to be unsuccessful, and the other is to be successful."

—*Oscar Wilde*

Chapter Two

THE LEADERSHIP SESSION
JANUARY, 1999

In a university commencement address several years ago, Brian Dyson, CEO of Coca Cola Enterprises, spoke of the relation of work to one's other commitments:

"Imagine life as a game in which you are juggling some five balls in the air. You name them—work, family, health, friends and spirit—and you're keeping all of these in the air. You will soon understand that work is a rubber ball. If you drop it, it will bounce back.

But the other four balls—family, health, friends and spirit are made of glass. If you drop one of these, they will be irrevocably scuffed, marked, nicked, damaged or even shattered. They will never be the same."

Author: Unknown
Source: Internet

"O'Hare—and quickly. I'm running late and my flight leaves in about 45 minutes," Briana yelled at the cab driver just outside her apartment on Waveland Avenue in Chicago.

It was a good thing, Briana thought, that she lived only a few blocks from Wrigley Field on one side and a few blocks from Lakeshore Drive on the other—cabs would not be hard to find.

What a way to spend a Sunday afternoon—off to Atlanta for a warm, fuzzy, three-day leadership training session. She was going to miss 'The Sopranos' and 'Sex in the City' on HBO—her favorite shows after Ally

McBeal. She pulled out the agenda she had just printed from her laptop—Iseus Tanga was the facilitator. Sounds foreign, she reflected nonchalantly.

"So wha' ya' think of Jordan retiring? I tell ya, this city ain't never gonna be da same. Pippen ain't gonna stick around neither—it's over—da Bulls is over," the driver blurted out.

"Looks like the whole NBA season is over. Have they settled the strike yet?" Briana asked.

"No, they're still striking. Millionaires striking? What's the world coming to? They elect Ventura Gov'ner of Minnesota—and then they break up da Bulls—it ain't right, I'm telling ya."

Briana looked out the window as they passed the skyline of downtown Chicago. She hated the winter but loved the city. It would have been nice to have kissed someone goodbye and have him waiting when she got back. There was an unsatisfactory emptiness growing in her heart that she was getting used to. Being a 38-year-old single female in this big city could be quite lonely. But she began to smile as she approached the airport and thought of her charming family and friends—she had the best of them. She coddled herself with the thought of her parents being married for 61 years and still living together in Mt. Vernon, New York. **There was always hope, even for a soul like hers, she mused.**

At about the same time, in Charlotte, North Carolina, Gabriel Sloan was kissing his wife, Heather, goodbye.

"I'll be back Thursday night," he promised.

"Drive carefully," Heather responded.

Gabe pulled out of his driveway just outside the Par-3 17th hole at the Highland Creek Golf Community in north Charlotte. He was about four miles from I-85, which he would take all the way to Atlanta for the same leadership training course as Briana. His boss, Joe Brathway, had insisted that all his superstars at the power company take this course.

Gabe was a 33-year-old, very intelligent, highly talented, overachieving and extremely ambitious professional engineer. **He was the type of person who refused to concede to life's challenges.** He marveled at his skills to 'make things happen.' Heather worked for a local bank as an account manager. Their marriage had been crumbling for a few years and Gabe did not seem aware of it.

As he turned onto the ramp for I-85, he put on his favorite CD—'Eric Clapton Unplugged'. His thoughts began to again wander back to Zambia, Africa.

Gabe's father was once a cartographer for National Geographic and moved to Zambia (Northern Rhodesia) after its independence from Britain in 1964 to map out most of its uncharted northern and western regions. Gabe went to school in Zambia until he was eighteen. He learned to speak many languages and although always considered 'a white foreigner' by the locals, he befriended many members of the various Zambian tribes. He taught himself to survive with very little.

Gabe had always had an antagonistic relationship with his family, especially with his father, who was constantly on the road in Zambia. Victor Sloan was an alcoholic and had a temper his family feared for most of their lives in Africa. Gabe was the third of four children. His mother, Norma, though still married to his father, had never been able to live outside the shadows of her husband's career and life. Gabe resented all the sacrifices his father forced the family to make. Gabe was well aware that a great deal of his sharply defined passion for success arose from a desire to prove to his father that he would be better than he—professionally and personally. Gabe was an avid reader and curious thinker—qualities that had always made him feel smarter than others.

At about the same time, just 20 miles northwest of downtown Atlanta, in Marietta, Georgia, the family of Alex and Olivia Montana was getting ready for dinner with their three children—Taylor, 7, John, 5, and little Lindsay, 3.

"Taylor—it's your turn to set the table!" screamed Olivia.

"Mom, can you get John to help? He is just playing Nintendo," Taylor fired back.

"I can help—let me help—I want to set the table," insisted little Lindsay.

"Lindsay, no! You broke two plates already—they're too big for you. Why don't you get the napkins from Daddy?" Olivia instructed.

"Hon, I gotta finish the burgers on the grill and it's cold out here. Keep Lindsay inside."

"Dad! Look! I'm winning! I'm winning!" John yelled with his eyes fixed on the TV and hands locked to the controls of the game.

Chaos. That was the word that Alex always used to describe his family dinners. But he loved it—every bit of it. Alex led a good life. His parents were his role models and they too lived in Atlanta, Georgia. He had no major skeletons in his closet, and his challenges were confined to balancing his professional career as Senior Manager in a Big 5 consulting firm called Impact Consulting. His job required 100% travel unless his projects were in Atlanta. He was well loved by his family and friends but, as his children continued to grow, he struggled painfully with the unyielding demands of his life and what ought to be important to him.

As the Montana family finally sat down at the table, Alex asked John to bless the food.

"Thank you God for the food and for the hands that prepared it also. Amen," John said, sending a grin to both Alex and Olivia's faces.

"What are you doing this week?" Olivia asked.

"Mom, I want more bread!" Taylor interrupted.

"No, Taylor—finish the two rolls you have on your plate first! I start some leadership training course tomorrow at the Marriott Marquis downtown. It's supposed to help us become leaders for the new millennium."

"Dad—what's mallanum?" Lindsay asked.

Alex looked at Olivia and realized they had agreed about four years ago to avoid having adult conversation at the dinner table with the kids. He smiled.

"May—Lay—Nee—Um. It's the year 2000," Olivia said slowly to Lindsay.

"Whose turn is it to put the kids in tonight?" Alex asked Olivia with a grin.

Fridays, Saturdays, and Sundays were Alex's days to manage the kids. That included karate class, T-ball league, soccer practice and games, bathing and putting the kids to bed. Olivia had the rest of the weekdays and nights so that Alex could focus on his blossoming career.

"What time does it start tomorrow?" Olivia asked.

"8:30AM—in the Grand Ballroom A."

The Leadership Session

Briana and Gabe stayed at the hotel and caught the same elevator from the 36th floor to the session on the ground floor. There were already about 30 people outside the ballroom getting coffee and munching on the traditional pastries, muffins, and bagels. It was about 8:20AM when Alex finally arrived—traffic. He quickly registered and grabbed his nametag.

At about 8:30, everyone began to file into the ballroom where about a hundred people were seated auditorium style. Alex, Briana, and Gabe all sat next to strangers and proceeded with the typical idle chat—"Hi, where are you from?"

"Good morning leaders of tomorrow!" came a voice from the podium up front.

It was a professorial-looking silver-haired man in his mid-50's, tall, slender, and dressed in a suit with a bow tie. He proceeded to give the following opening remarks:

My name is Darryl Bond—no relation to James. (chuckle- chuckle!)

Let's start by saying goodbye to the Industrial Economy and saying hello to the Opportunistic Knowledge-Based economy. Say goodbye to the Expert Model and hello to the Team Model. Say goodbye to management as you have known it and hello to the management that will constantly change. In the 1970's, when I was getting into management, the model was the country club, hierarchical, command and control model.

In the '80s, it began to change to TQM (Total Quality Management) and in the '90s it is the teams and process-efficiencies model. Tomorrow, in your world, the focus will be on transient and virtual work-based teams—real-time decision-making in a growingly complex operating environment with an unprecedented level of diversity in everything you do. Your bosses will not be able to help you; they have no context or reference for what you are managing. What you need will be each other—your professional support network within your level and your ability to teach and learn from each other on the same day will be your greatest asset. This will comprise the so-called 'Emergent Structure'—the unprinted organizational model that will tell you where to go and what to do to get things accomplished.

Recently, I reviewed the results of internal HR surveys of many of the companies you represent. Across the board, employee satisfaction dropped significantly when your demographic, the managers, was analyzed. What is it about your phase in the professional career path that troubles you? Why are you unhappy?

I have traveled extensively and read a great deal. I can tell you that you are arguably, and ironically enough, the luckiest generation of human beings ever to have walked the face of this earth. So, let's see if we can figure this one out together.

You are a new generation of managers in a $30 trillion world economy. You have come from all over the country to this unique three-day session. You will all be randomly separated into groups of nine. On the third day you will form teams of three that you will keep in touch with for the rest of the year. This small group will be your designated network—the three will become your professional buddies—you will coach each other for the next 10 months until we all meet again in Miami in December. You will be given a guide for the year—a facilitator who will help you process and document your experiences.

The next three days, and indeed the rest of the year, are designed to teach you about the one person you need to become most familiar with—yourself. As a leader, all your strengths and weaknesses will be challenged—this I assure you.

I quote Bob Pritchard: "When you're not learning—someone somewhere else is. When you meet—guess who has the advantage?"

I would characterize your leadership journey not only as one that is beginning, but also one where the rules of the game will have changed considerably by the time you're done.

So go forth, leaders of tomorrow, for tomorrow will be here much sooner than you expect.

With that, Darryl Bond walked off the stage. People in the audience looked at each other somewhat bewildered and then slowly, as though rehearsed, began applauding.

A young lady came to the podium next and instructed the participants to proceed to their respective breakout rooms.

"Wow! That was quick," Briana said to the man next to her.

"Yeah—I hope the next three days are quick too," he replied.

Briana was disappointed with his cheap gibe and secretly hoped he would not be in her breakout session. Alex was encouraged with the unique start. Gabe seemed to be preparing for a challenge.

"Wisdom is the power to put our time and our knowledge to the proper use."

—Thomas Watson

Chapter Three

THE BREAKOUT SESSION

"Our deepest fear is not that we are inadequate. Our deepest fear is that we are powerful beyond measure. It is our light, not our darkness, that most frightens us. We ask ourselves, who am I to be brilliant, gorgeous, talented, and fabulous? Actually, who are you not to be? ... Your playing small does not serve the world. There is nothing enlightening about shrinking, so that other people won't feel insecure around you. We are born to make manifest the glory...that is within us. It is not just in some of us; it is in everyone. And as we let our light shine, we unconsciously give other people permission to do the same. As we are liberated from our own fear, our presence automatically liberates others."

Excerpt from Nelson Mandela's 1994 inaugural speech
Source: Internet

Gabe and Alex arrived at their room, The Sydney Room, at the same time. The room had three small round tables. Briana followed next and joined Alex and Gabe as their third member. Others slowly trickled in.

"Hi, I'm Briana Jones, from St. Peter's Hospital in Chicago."

"I'm Gabe Sloan, with Charlotte Power and Light in Charlotte."

"And I'm Alex Montana, with Impact Consulting, right here in Atlanta."

The three all nodded politely as they introduced themselves.

"Good morning everyone. Please be seated quickly so we can get started. My name is Iseus Tanga—I'm from La Jolla, just outside of San Diego. Today and tomorrow you will spend in this room, and the third and final day you will spend with your group of three developing plans and ground rules for the next 10 months. Most of your time will be interactive—I will learn from you and you will learn from me.

Let's start with an exercise. In front of each of you are three cards—each card is individually labeled with Money or Respect or Knowledge".

At this point, take a piece of paper and tear it into three pieces. Label each piece Money, Knowledge, and Respect.

"Listen carefully. I want you to look at these three cards and think about what they mean to you. Then throw two away and keep the one dearest to you."

Briana looked at Alex and frowned. This was odd, they thought.

Follow similar instructions and part with two.

Gabe was quick to react and quickly tore up the Money and Respect cards. Briana was pensive but eventually parted with Money and Respect also. Alex looked at his cards and thought about his father. He instantly knew he wanted respect and so parted with Knowledge and Money.

What did you chose and why?

_____

_____

"Okay," Iseus declared after a few minutes, "Tell me what you chose and why."

All nine in the room got up and shared their reasons for settling on the card they had refused to part with. Only one person had kept money. His logic was that money would extend to him the opportunity to gain knowledge and respect. The rest, with the exception of Alex, chose Knowledge. Knowledge, they argued, would lead to all the money and respect one would need. Alex contended that all the money and knowledge in the world was useless if one did not have the respect of family, friends, and peers.

After the entire group answered, Iseus paused, then calmly said, "You have all fallen into the old paradigm of management. And one you will have to break out of very quickly. **The right answer was all three or even two—not one.**"

"Whoa there, Mr. Seus—you said chose one," a participant quickly reminded Iseus.

"The name is pronounced Ee-Zay-Os, not Seus. Why did you listen to me? All of you said that you wanted all three and even argued over which one would best get to the other two."

"But we were following instructions," Gabe reminded Iseus.

"And by doing so you compromised the strong rival voice in your heart that kept saying you wanted all three. **You accepted the enacted limitations placed on you by some stranger with a strange name without challenging him. As leaders, your first lesson is to listen to and trust your rationalization.** Think around the ostensible barriers that life erects in front of you."

There was a long introspective pause in the room. Iseus' exercise had clearly met their burden of proof.

How good are you at taking what someone has given you and thinking outside of the proverbial box? What do you think are the reasons for this?

"I wanted to start with this exercise to let you know that you are free to think for yourselves. I've only been alive once and I don't know anyone who has done this living thing twice. The wisdom is in this room, as they say. I urge you to challenge everything and make sure it makes sense to you. Make sure it feels right and make sure you listen to the little voice in the back of your head. As leaders, **you must embrace all obstacles as opportunities to be creative.**"

Describe an experience in the last two years that forced you to be creative with unplanned constraints.

_____

_____

_____

"He's good," Gabe acknowledged to Briana and Alex.

"Okay—let's commit to challenging everything," Briana whispered with a smile.

The little voice in all their heads told them they would get along just fine with Iseus. He sharply contrasted with their image of a management coach, but his first exercise was an 'aha' moment they appreciated.

Iseus, as he insisted on being called, proceeded to set up some ground rules. Confidentiality between the groups was critical, and he made the group sign confidentiality forms that were submitted not to him, but to each other.

He then asked the participants to take a full hour and formally introduce themselves to each other answering the following questions:

Write down your personal information in the lines provided.

• *Name and occupation*

_____

_____

• *Family background*

_____

_____

_____

- *Your strengths*

  _____

  _____

  _____

- *Your weaknesses*

  _____

  _____

- *Your aspirations for the next year*

  _____

  _____

  _____

- *2 key influencers of your life*

  _____

  _____

Gabe broke the ice. He was a little uncomfortable with sharing this type of information—he had never really put too much thought into it. But he figured he had nothing to lose.

Gabe said he was a Senior Project Manager (SPM) and a civil engineer by trade. He was responsible for about 40 people in his Highway Design Department. He was responsible for coordinating multiple teams like the Specifications Team, the Design Team, the Approval (regulatory) Team, the Print/Reproduction Team, and the Construction Team. His clients were developers and real estate financial institutions.

Gabe told Alex and Briana about his family background and how he had spent 18 years in southern Africa in Zambia. As far as strengths, he considered himself to be technical, intuitive and very good with people. He said he was the youngest SPM to be a Department Head and had no doubt he would be promoted in two years to Vice President. Gabe said his weakness was the internal rancor in his life—he was black and white about people and decisions. If someone were to stab him in the back, he was very vindictive and never forgot an enemy. His goal for the next year was to establish himself as the best SPM in the company, and to make his group the most profitable one. Gabe hesitated as he spoke of his influencers, but said they were his mother and a mentor he met early in his professional career.

"What about your wife? You didn't mention her at all," Briana asked.

Gabe was quiet. Briana could not tell if she had offended him.

"We're here to learn and everything is confidential—what do we have to lose?" Alex said calmly.

"Well, we're happy, but she has her career at the bank and we let each other pursue our dreams. We don't have children, if that's what you're asking," Gabe answered tritely.

Briana went next. She really wanted to let her hair down and take advantage of this session. Her instinct told her that she probably would never see Alex and Gabe again.

She began by revealing that she was single and had never been married. She told Alex and Gabe about her parents' 61-year-old marriage. She said she was well loved by her family, her extended family, and had numerous friends. She added that she enjoyed her life and had worked extremely hard the past 10 years. She went back to a community college when she was 26, and then on to the University of Wisconsin where she graduated Cum Laude in 1990.

Briana characterized her job as the Chief Administrator of several wings at St. Peter's Hospital in Chicago. She lived by herself in a small apartment just a few blocks away from Wrigley Field, she continued, to which Alex and Gabe both responded by saying they had always wanted to go to Wrigley Field. Her most significant regret, as a 38-year-old woman, was that she did not have the family she always had presumed she would have had by now. She often felt that she might never have children and that was a source of great anxiety.

Her strengths included her great devotion to her work. She managed about 150 nurses at the hospital. Her department was 24/7—which meant it functioned 24 hours a day for 7 days a week. She conceded that her true passion was teaching dance to little children and wished she could make the same money teaching children that she made with her current job. She also loved meeting new and different people and was always rated as an excellent manager. She suggested her weaknesses to be her infuriation with the stereotype people had of older, single women. She confessed that she also did not deal very well with too much change. Her goal for the coming year was to spend more time volunteering with Girl University in Chicago, where she could teach more children how to dance. Her two influences were her family support system and a priest from the Catholic Church, Father Andreas, whom she had met some 12 years ago. She said she missed her hometown in New York and would like to eventually return there.

"Well, why haven't you been married? Were you ever engaged?" Gabe asked.

"Once. I was engaged when I was 30 to a great guy. He was right for everyone, but something in my heart told me he was not my life partner and I did not want to compromise my destiny. It was the right decision."

Gabe nodded, realizing Briana was a very intelligent, smart, and passionate human being.

Alex went next and said that he too had a great family support network in Atlanta, and that he was very happy with his career as Senior Manager at Impact Consulting. He told Briana and Gabe about Olivia and his three adorable children. His only challenge was to keep a healthy balance between his career aspirations, which included becoming a partner in the firm in the next three years, and his family. He did not want to cheat his children nor himself out of the many life experiences that fathers traditionally had with their children.

Alex espoused his main strength to be his calmness—he rarely lost his composure. He also said that he thought matters through quite thoroughly before reacting. His weaknesses, he suggested, were that he was risk averse and conflict averse. He detested fighting battles—and playing the necessary office politics—and would rather concede than fight one. His goal was to spend as much time with his family while maintaining his career path. He said he was going to be assigned to a project in Dallas, Texas, in a couple of weeks and was not looking forward to it. His major influences were clearly his parents.

Take your responses to the above six questions and insert them in the designated sections of the picture below. This is your hut. You will need this for proceeding exercises.

1.   *Strengths and weaknesses in the foundation*
2.   *Influences in the door*
3.   *Family background in the window*
4.   *Aspirations in the roof*

Your Hut

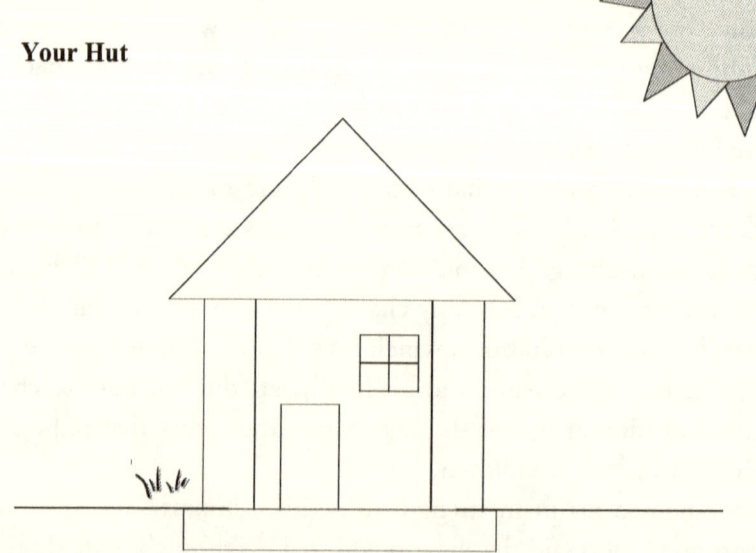

After a short break, Iseus began to introduce himself. He said his father was from the Middle East and his mother was from Turkey. He was raised in Alexandria, Egypt, but traveled a good bit with his father who worked for the Red Cross. He got into the business of leadership development and executive coaching after he realized human beings were not a closed system—they were inherently incapable of separating themselves into 'professionals' at one moment and 'personal' at another, he submitted. The wealth of experiences he had had across the world taught him how to thrive at being himself as well as how to weave in spirituality at any age or stage of life. It was astonishing to him, he said, **that people in America had little semblance of how lucky they were to be living in a free country.** The abundance of choice and the availability of products and services in the U.S. was stunning. He said it still shocked him to go to a grocery store in La Jolla and see all the shelves fully stocked—not feeling like he had to bribe someone to get milk or a loaf of bread. He said he could walk or drive just about anywhere and not feel threatened that he would be shot at or apprehended because of his race or level in society. He had spent the last 10 years working with executives from all over the country helping them unravel their greatest mysteries—themselves. He found that in helping them existentially recognize themselves, these executives had become much better people and, in turn, significantly better leaders.

Briana, Gabe, and Alex were all very intrigued by this strange man. Iseus was no more than five feet tall, slender, and tan-skinned. In a sure-fire way, there was something about him, they all felt, that was special. Not in a prophetic sense, but in a very spiritual and paradoxically simple way.

Iseus began to draw on the flipcharts, "The second foundation exercise we will do is called "La Maison De Sebastien" or in English—Sebastian's House. It is a metaphor we will all use very often—I assure you this. So pay attention."

Iseus drew a picture of a house—a square with a triangle on top of it. He said living the days of our lives was analogous to building a house and each experience was like a single brick in the house. Once something is experienced, once a brick is laid, Iseus argued, it could never be removed. **It may be altered, disguised, replaced by a similar brick—but the original occupant of that time in the construction of one's home, one's life, will forever leave an imprint.**

The group was noticeably engaged.

"The foundation of a house is its core—its strength and its weakness, depending on how it was built. **Similarly, the early experiences of your life form your core (your formative years) and they are either your strength or your weakness depending on the experience.** Experiences that resulted in emotional trauma, if not dealt with, tend to be weaknesses, and those that resulted in love and compassion tend to be strengths."

"Wait a minute, Iseus—I'd like to challenge that," Gabe interrupted. "I had some challenging experiences in Africa when I was a kid, but today those very experiences are my strengths—they give me reason to wake up every morning and prove to the world that I am a worthy participant in the evolution of my race."

"What is your gift to this world?" Iseus asked Gabe.

What do you consider your gift to the world to be?

_____

_____

_____

Gabe was reflective. And so was everyone else. A full minute went by and still no reaction from anyone. The tone of the session had abruptly changed.

"I guess my gift to this world is the wisdom of my experiences. My experiences give me clarity and I guess I bring that clarity to my work," Gabe finally responded.

"Who have you changed and made better, Gabe? What have you changed and made better? What about you makes everyone else around you feel special about themselves?" Iseus asked boldly but calmly.

Answer the same questions for yourself.

_____

_____

Another long pause ensued.

"I am making a living and supporting my family. I was not made to save the world. The world screwed me and life owes me the success I am enjoying," Gabe muttered back.

"All of you—take the next 15 minutes and write down what your passion is," Iseus instructed.

What is your passion in life?

_____

_____

_____

After a few minutes, some of the people at the other tables raised their hands.

"Iseus, **I think one of the problems here is that most of us don't know what our passion is.** I am 28 years old and I've never really thought about it. I think people that know their passion are like people who are in love—they are just lucky. I mean, I know the adage that if you follow your passion you'll never have to work a single day in your life—that's just in the movies," one said.

"Passion," Iseus said slowly. "I love that word. We were supposed to do this activity tomorrow—but let's do it now since we are ready for it. I am passing out these worksheets. Fill them out individually and I will come and help you figure out what your passion is."

In the first column, describe three different experiences in your life, three bricks in the construction of your house, that gave you the greatest sense of pride and accomplishment. They can be personal or professional experiences and it does not matter how old you were when you experienced them. Once you have written your three experiences, then respond to each of the four additional questions."

Complete this matrix for yourself.

Experiences	What was your role?	Who was it for?	What were the specific outcomes?	What did you feel?(list emotions)
Brick 1				
Brick 2				
Brick 3				

The exercise proved to be much more challenging than the group initially anticipated. Iseus walked around the room and talked to each person. Although it was very quiet in the room, every mind in the room was hard at work deliberating with their memories.

Alex, Briana, and Gabe all filled out their matrices.

Below is one experience, or brick, from each one of them:

Experiences	What was your role?	Who was it for?	What were the specific outcomes?	What did you feel? (list emotions)
ALEX I helped my son figure out how to throw a baseball straight to somebody else	I was the instructor	My son. He had nothing to offer me except a personal satisfaction of my having passed on something my dad taught me	John is now playing shortstop in T-ball league and loves every minute of it	Pride Joy Satisfaction Envy Happiness Accomplishment
BRIANA We had a major systems implementation that took over 6 months and over 30 people. We worked our rear ends off and sacrificed personal time	I was the team leader and provided day-to-day strategic direction for the team	St. Peter's Hospital but ultimately, it was for all the nurses, doctors and staff of the hospital who now had real time & accessible information	We were on time; everyone appreciated what we did and I made sure the team was rewarded handsomely	Pride Joy Satisfaction Happiness Accomplishment
GABE My department had the highest profit margin last year – we made 24% when the average was 11%	I was the leader	The company	My team and I got the highest bonuses last year and we are all viewed as the cash cow department of the company	Victorious Winners

Once the matrix had been filled out, Iseus asked everyone to find a common theme to each one of the four questions on the experiences. What were the common emotions? What roles were they playing in the bricks? What role did they want to play? Who was around? Who was not around? What was **really** needed in each brick?

To everyone's surprise, this was much easier. In fact, the themes stuck out with a dazzling glare. Iseus explained that the themes represented clues to one's passion. If one were to seek experiences, jobs, people, spouses, relationships, that allowed one to manifest these clues, then one would be pursuing one's passion. The challenge, Iseus said, was to have the fortitude and moxie to walk away from experiences that were not capable of allowing one to exhibit any of these clues (common themes).

List your common themes from each question:

What was your role?

_____

_____

Who was it for?

_____

_____

What were the specific outcomes?

_____

_____

What did you feel (list emotions)?

_____

_____

What do you think your passion is now?

_____

_____

If it is different from what you initially thought it was (page 33), why do you think it is different now?

_____

_____

What kinds of jobs/roles do you think would best manifest your passion?

_____

_____

Transfer your passion statement above into the sun in the picture of your hut.

Iseus went back to his flip chart of Sebastien's House. He said that in every house, in every life, some loose brick had been laid. **He defined loose bricks as experiences that have not been processed, experiences that are often repressed.** He said he could map out and trace every subsequent experience in our lives to one or more of these loose bricks. These loose bricks would determine how steady and robust a house would be in its ability to withstand a natural challenge, like a hurricane. **Similarly, Iseus argued, one's intrinsic loose bricks would determine one's ability to endure the challenges of life and enable one to react in a manner that would not cause anyone any harm.**

It was time for lunch.

"In the afternoon we will dig deeper and get to know ourselves a little bit better. And start thinking about your loose bricks," Iseus concluded.

Alex, Briana, and Gabe all stood up and stretched.

"This stuff is exhausting," Alex confessed.

"No kidding," Gabe agreed.

"I wonder what we'll do in the afternoon?" Briana asked.

While Gabe and Briana joined the buffet line, Alex called Olivia from his mobile phone to check on her and the kids.

"You can't build a reputation on what you are going to do...Do it now!"

—Anonymous

Chapter Four

LEAVING ATLANTA—BACK TO THE REAL WORLD

One day an expert in time management was speaking to a group of business students and, to drive home a point, used an illustration those students would never forget. As he stood in front of the group of high-powered overachievers, he said, "Okay, time for a quiz." Then he pulled out a one-gallon, wide mouthed Mason jar and set it on the table in front of him.

Then he produced about a dozen fist-sized rocks and carefully placed them, one at a time, into the jar. When the jar was filled to the top and no more rocks would fit inside, he asked, "Is this jar full?"

Everyone in the class said, "Yes." Then he said, "Really?" He reached under the table and pulled out a bucket of gravel. Then he dumped some gravel in and shook the jar causing pieces of gravel to work themselves down into the space between the big rocks. Then he asked the group once more, "Is the jar full?"

By this time, the class was on to him. "Probably not," one of them answered.

"Good!" he replied. He reached under the table and brought out a bucket of sand. He started dumping the sand in the jar and it went into all of the spaces left between the rocks and the gravel. Once more he asked the question, "Is this jar full?"

"No!" the class shouted. Once again, he said, "Good." Then he grabbed a pitcher of water and began to pour it in until the jar was filled to the brim. Then he looked at the class and asked, "What is the point of this illustration?" One eager beaver raised his hand and said, "The point is, no matter how full your schedule is, if you try really hard you can always fit some more things in it."

"No," the speaker replied, "That's not the point. The truth this illustration teaches us is: if you don't put the big rocks in first, you'll never get them in at all."

What are the big rocks in your life? Your children: your loved ones, your education, your dreams, a worthy cause, teaching or mentoring others, doing things that you love, time to yourself, your health, your significant other. Remember to put these BIG ROCKS in first or you'll never get them in at all. If you sweat the little stuff (the gravel, the sand) then you'll fill your life with little things you worry about that don't really matter, and you'll never have the real quality time you need to spend on the big, important stuff (the big rocks).

Author: Unknown
Source: Internet

"So, you think Atlanta and the 'Dirty Birds' have a shot at beating Elway and the Broncos next week?" Gabe asked Alex during lunch.

"Go Falcons, baby!" Alex declared.

"Have you guys seen 'Patch Adams' yet? My girlfriends and I saw it last weekend and it was great. Iseus kinda reminds me of him a little," Briana observed.

"I haven't seen a movie in a theater in over two years—I think 'Titanic' was the last movie we saw. Kids….," Alex responded.

"Heather, my wife, wanted to see that last weekend but I had golf with the guys and she went with her friends. She didn't tell me what she thought of it," Gabe said, acting somewhat surprised.

Iseus was standing in front of the room next to his flipcharts when his nine managers returned. On the flipchart was a huge "$100" sign.

"Imagine you have $100 each day as Emotional Energy. **You begin each day with $100 and you have the option of using as much or as little of it each day, but you can't carry anything left over to the next day. The** money is spent on tasks and activities that require emotional energy from you. If, for example, you have a big performance meeting with your boss at 10AM, and it does not go well, then I suspect you will use all of your $100 by lunchtime. This means that whatever happens after lunch, you will exercise the least amount of collegiality, tolerance, patience, and wisdom. On the other hand, if the meeting goes very well, you may actually increase your $100 of emotional energy and exhibit more patience in the afternoon. The $100 is a metaphor for a tank of positive energy that can be depleted by experiences that wear us out emotionally or repleted by experiences that make us feel worthy. Any questions on this simple concept?" Iseus asked.

Iseus asked the class to imagine a typical week or day in their lives, both personally and professionally. Then he asked them to complete the following sheet:

On a typical workday, list the people that give you emotional energy and attach a dollar value to each person. Total should not exceed $100.

Name	Amount
Total	$100

On a typical workday, list the tasks and activities that give you emotional energy and attach a dollar value to each task. Total should not exceed $100.

Task	Amount

———————————————

———————————————

Total $100

Compare these activities with your passion in your hut. Any observations?

———————————————

———————————————

On a typical workday, list the people that deplete you of emotional energy and attach a dollar value to each person. Total should not exceed $100.

Name	Amount
Total	$100

On a typical workday, list the tasks that deplete you of emotional energy and attach a dollar value to each task. Total should not exceed $100.

Task	Amount
Total	$100

Iseus then asked the group to discuss the results in their three-member groups. Briana, Alex, and Gabe had begun to bond. They were surprised at how quickly they trusted each other. Even Gabe was beginning to share more about himself. They spent about an hour discussing each other's answers and asking probing questions. The small group allowed for good quality interaction that created a captivating hunger for more in the participants.

For Gabe, it was the people in the other departments, the 'slackers' he called them, that constituted the lion's share of his energy depletion. He did not enjoy working with them and particularly resented the fact that they were riding his coattails because of his department's financial success. Gabe thoroughly enjoyed his troops, his employees. They were all intensely productive, very loyal to him, and would do anything to remain a part of his winning team.

Alex said his repletion of energy came from his family. He loved them. They made him happy and even made a dismal day at work bearable. The politics of work at the consulting firm drained Alex—this was something he was not good at nor did he know how to become so. He watched people who were great at being diplomatic and building strong relationships with people that could ultimately help them advance in their careers. Alex simply did not know how to relentlessly pursue schmoozing. After work, Alex typically wanted to go home to his family, while his peers went out to restaurants and bars to socialize and build strong networks. They would do anything to gallop ahead of the pack, but Alex did not envy them.

Conflict was one thing Briana hated—she dreaded having to confront one of the nurses or staff on her ward. But, ironically, she was always applauded for how she handled confrontations. She said she would always check and double-check her facts before any meeting so she would not lose her composure. She thoroughly enjoyed some of the nurses, who were her close friends, and looked forward to Tuesday and Thursday nights when she taught dance to little girls at Girl University.

"Remember this exercise and the $100. We will use it to prioritize activities in our days and weeks. As leaders, doing this should become second nature to you," Iseus said.

"You are saying we should enjoy everything we do? I mean, that's just not realistic. In every workday we have to do things that aren't fun—that's life," someone from another table stated.

"That is true—but **recognize that those things deplete you of your $100 and plan your day accordingly so that you can either schedule activities that replete you or that you don't plan any major events that require your total and objective frame of mind once you've had a significant depletion**," Iseus replied.

"Good point," Briana nodded.

"Let's return to those bricks now and begin to put the pieces together," said Iseus.

He began to talk about loose bricks again and said one had to figure out what those loose bricks are. **Humans, he submitted, fear what they do not understand much more than what they do not know, and exhibiting behavior that one does not understand is a massive self-esteem killer.** It forces people to become cautious and apprehensive instead of reflective and instinctive. Most people do not have a framework in which to process their behavior or that of others. Sebastien's House, Iseus contended, is such a framework.

"I want you to think about your loose bricks," Iseus said softly. "I want you to think of your life before you left home; for most of you that would be around eighteen. Think of your loose bricks and write down for yourselves only what three of them are. You will not be asked to share this with anyone," Iseus instructed.

"Can you give us a better understanding or an example of a loose brick?" Briana asked.

"**Trust, effort, and love.** Think of times when you either demonstrated these or expected these three self-actualizing needs. **Your loose bricks would be experiences when these three elements were significantly violated.** I'll give you a personal example: when I was 14 and living in Turkey, a war broke out and I witnessed people, ordinary people, do things to other people that are unthinkable. I never knew a human being was capable of so much evil and destruction. That experience shattered my faith and my trust in anyone for about 20 years. Because I knew what people were capable of doing, I was never able to get close enough to trust them with something important—I was a general—I liked to control everything. By controlling everything, I left little room for people to disappoint me or, as it turns out, to amaze me," Iseus responded.

Iseus' disclosure was encouraging and affirming. It was very quiet in the room again. It was amazing how he was able to make everyone feel so comfortable. That little voice in the back of Briana's, Gabe's, and Alex's heads was reinforcing their faith in him as someone they could learn a great deal from. He was humble, this foreign man, and though very feeble in appearance, he had a distinguishing aura of strength. Briana was glad that he would be their coach in the coming months.

List three loose bricks in your life.

1. _____
   _____
   _____

2. _____
   _____
   _____

3. _____
   _____
   _____

Write a short phrase to describe each of your loose bricks and transfer that phrase to the yard area of your hut on page 30.

Gabe, Briana, and Alex wrote at length about their loose bricks. Gabe's bricks were all laid in Africa and involved his alcoholic father. Alex knew what his were but was too afraid to write them down. He had not thought of those experiences for many years but he felt that now might be the time.

He was a father now and the demands from his firm were growing exponentially. He knew he could not wait much longer; he wanted and needed the freedom from it. Alex did not write anything down. Briana's bricks were not centered around her family—but on an eating disorder. Her family had a vivid notion of perfection and physical appearance had a great deal to do with it. She always tried to be that perfect person for them.

Iseus then asked the class to review some of the earlier worksheets they had worked on. He asked the class to look at their loose bricks and compare them in tandem to the activities that cost more than $10 of their emotional energy. Then he instructed them to list the common emotions from both experiences.

Make a list of the common emotions from your energy depletions and your loose bricks.

_____

_____

_____

What conclusions can you draw from these common emotions?

_____

_____

_____

How might these estranged emotions play out in other parts of your life?

_____

_____

_____

"Iseus, I have my common emotions. For example, in my loose bricks, I could not trust people to come through for me and I hated that. In my depletions, I hate waiting on people to deliver also. But are you saying that by realizing what these common emotions are we can avoid them altogether?" Gabe asked.

"No. I'm saying first you must comprehend what you don't understand—and now at least you understand what the root causes of your current behaviors are. And for the next few months, I want you all to think about your loose bricks every time you exhibit behavior that you either don't understand or think you need to change. As a leader, it is not enough to have a reason for just yourself—you will need to work with all types of people and if you truly want to be successful, and happy with your success, then you will have to exploit your creative energy and teach yourself how to diplomatically ask what other people's bricks are. Then you will be able to comprehend why they are behaving the way they are. If you can do that, you will be able to lead more than just one department, Gabe; you will be able to lead all of Charlotte Power and Light. And better yet, all of Charlotte Power and Light will want you to lead them."

Gabe looked at Iseus. This time he was not surprised. He was in thought, deep thought.

"It's hard to peel the onion to see what a person's potential is. I tend to focus on what they can do for me now, not tomorrow, when they have figured out how to add value. By then, it's too late," Gabe fretted.

Iseus quickly turned to his flipchart and drew the figure (#1) below. He drew three; one for each table and asked the class to transform the stick figure into their image of a perfect employee. He promised this was not a trick question like the Money-Knowledge-Respect exercise.

Figure 1

On the image above, use your pencil/pen and draw your picture of a perfect worker.

Gabe, Briana, and Alex began to draw their ideal worker. Gabe wanted a suit on the figure so that he would look professional.

"Does it have to be man, Gabe? Why can't it be a woman or a unisex person?" Briana asked rather seriously.

"You're right. I work with mostly men and immediately thought of a suit. My bad. Let's just draw nice clothes on the person and a briefcase."

"How about big ears to show they're good listeners?" Alex suggested.

"And draw a heart on their chest to show they are thoughtful and considerate of other people," Briana added.

The drawing continued for almost ten minutes. Finally, Iseus asked each team to present its perfect employee. Alex presented his group's output. They were all fairly similar in their characteristics.

Then Iseus drew the same stick figure on a blank flipchart (#2) and asked them to look at it closely. Then, quietly, he asked, "Why would this be the perfect employee?"

Figure 2

Everyone in the class abruptly paused in reaction to the question Iseus posed. And quietly, they all agreed. **It was apparent that all their additions to the figure were of intrinsic qualities that were not outwardly visible.**

"As leaders," Iseus said, "it is imperative that you not compromise the capabilities of your employees by their appearance. That would be true myopia. **Leaders should be willing to 'peel the onion' and be wrong about some people.** They would be surprised, at how many people would rise to the occasion given the opportunity," he continued.

"So what do you think it is that we, managers, need ourselves? I mean, we're in the middle of all this. We have bosses with high expectations and we have employees that are also demanding. I can't wait to get out of this phase in my career, to be totally honest with you, Iseus," someone from another table commented.

"All our research indicates that there are two motivating factors that drive everyone in this room. First is a **sense of progress**; you need to know that whatever it is you are doing is leading to something better. That something better could be more knowledge, more responsibility, a raise, a promotion—anything. You must force yourself to sit down with your boss or mentor at least twice a year and get a sense of the progress you are making in your career and your life.

Secondly, you **need to feel like you are contributing** and adding to the value-chain of your business. In smaller companies, it is easier to get big accounts and more responsibilities and feel valued, needed, and appreciated. In larger companies, no matter how savvy you are, it is easy to get lost by merely being a number. This is why the dot coms are attractive to so many of you—they are relatively small and you are in start-up mode where everything you do literally adds value and progress and is tangible and measurable.

But remember, as these dot coms grow, they become aware that they lack processes, organizational models, and efficiencies that will very soon have to be installed, and then it's back to the large company mode. Then it is not as much fun anymore. In large workforces, the boundaries of what you are supposed to do and what you're not is unclear. The training manuals don't quite cover day-to-day challenges in this environment. Here, rewards systems can be confusing—how some people get rewarded is baffling.

In the '70s and '80s, the dot coms were cable and wireless companies. Young, competent, ambitious, and entrepreneurial professionals like you were thrilled at the opportunity. Today, these companies are like any other big company—looking for efficiencies everywhere," Iseus commented.

"I don't understand why corporate America can't take advantage of this spirit of ambition and entrepreneurship we have. They could make millions off us. If I ran several of the departments, I guarantee you I could turn them around in a year," Gabe contended.

"Wall Street looks at corporate America everyday and the pressures of capitalism, generating value, are enormous. Your bosses get measured on this. They are forced to think short term most of the time. And they hire people to do a job—to baby sit and not help share a sense of progress and contribution. This is where they have surely missed the boat. **They have not figured out that every company's cash cow is indeed their management, that if they nurtured and developed this group, not only would they be enormously profitable, but they would create an equitable succession planning model that would allow them to retire quite comfortably.** It is a delicate balance that few leaders are willing to pioneer," Iseus said.

"You should get our bosses to come to these sessions, Iseus," someone in the class uttered sarcastically.

"The only difference between your situation and theirs when they were managers is the **pace of change**—nothing else. They, too, wrestled with your challenges, but they did not have as many options as you do today. I know many of them think your generation is not as loyal as they were, but it could easily be argued that companies are also not as loyal to employees as they once were, and that weighing one's option and changing jobs several times is simply following an opportunity that will lead to a personal sense of progress, contribution, and good business acumen," Iseus concluded.

Write down what you think are the major differences between you and your boss. Respond in terms of style, values, work ethic, priorities, skill, competency, and vision.

_____

_____

_____

_____

_____

Write down what you think are the major misconceptions your leadership has of management (or employees at your level).

_____

_____

_____

_____

_____

The following day was similar to the first. Iseus continued to challenge how the class rationalized through challenges and the class was responding to him remarkably well. The bond between Iseus and the class members was undoubtedly getting stronger.

On the third and final day, Gabe, Alex, and Briana met only as a small group. Iseus spent only an hour in the morning and another in the afternoon with them. The three agreed to conference call each other every two weeks on Wednesday afternoons at 2PM EST. Briana agreed to coordinate the first few calls. They also agreed to be there if any one of them needed just-in-time support or a sounding board. They were all pleasantly surprised at the past three days. It was unlike any other training course they had been to and they were looking forward to charting each other's progress.

Alex insisted on driving Briana to the airport. Gabe began his four hour drive back to Charlotte at about 4PM.

He had meant to call Heather and tell her he was coming home that day (Wednesday) and not Thursday as he had originally planned. But Gabe was feeling so much better about himself than he had in a long time that he thought he would surprise Heather. He even stopped in Greenville and bought her flowers. He needed to pay attention to all of his life, he realized. As he kept driving, he pondered the many questions Iseus' exercises posed.

At about 9PM, as Briana was opening her apartment door in Chicago, and as Alex and Olivia had just finished putting the kids to bed in Atlanta, Gabe pulled into his driveway in Charlotte. There was an unfamiliar silver BMW in the driveway. Gabe was surprised but he proceeded to his back yard entrance as he normally did and entered his home. He immediately heard laughter. He began to think the worst. His blood was racing through his body as he slowly and reluctantly followed the laughter to their bedroom. What he saw next was every husband's worst nightmare.

*"Creative minds always have been known
to survive any kind of bad training."*

—Anna Freud

Chapter Five

THE EMOTIONAL THEORY OF RELAVITY
SPRING, 1999

In his book, Bill Gates talks about how feel-good, politically correct teachings created a full generation of kids with no concept of reality and how this concept set them up for failure in the real world. Here's an excerpt:

RULE 1   Life is not fair; get used to it.

RULE 2   The world won't care about your self-esteem. The world will expect you to accomplish something BEFORE you feel good about yourself.

RULE 3   You will NOT make 40 thousand dollars a year right out of high school. You won't be a vice president with a car phone, until you earn both.

RULE 4   If you think your teacher is tough, wait until you get a boss. He doesn't have tenure.

RULE 5   Flipping burgers is not beneath your dignity. Your grandparents had a different word for burger flipping; they called it opportunity.

RULE 6   If you mess up, it's not your parents' fault, so don't whine about your mistakes, learn from them.

RULE 7　Before you were born, your parents weren't as boring as they are now. They got that way from paying your bills, cleaning your clothes and listening to you talk about how cool you are. So before you save the rain forest from the parasites of your parents' generation, try "delousing" the closet in your own room.

RULE 8　Your school may have done away with winners and losers, but life has not. In some schools they have abolished failing grades; they'll give you as many times as you want to get the right answer. This doesn't bear the slightest resemblance to ANYTHING in real life.

RULE 9　Life is not divided into semesters. You don't get summers off and very few employers are interested in helping you find yourself. Do that on your own time.

RULE 10　Television is NOT real life. In real life people actually have to leave the coffee shop and go to jobs.

Author: Bill Gates
Source: Internet

"Looks like the trial is finally over," Alex whispered to Olivia as they prepared for bed.

"Al, I am so tired of hearing about Clinton and Monica and these senators acting like they have an ounce of moral fiber in them. It's ridiculous," Olivia responded. "By the way, where are you going to be this week?"

"Dallas again. I will be there through Thursday night."

"The kids are really beginning to miss you. At dinner, they keep asking where you are eating and what you are eating. They are so cute. It's hard for me to control them by myself. And John's ear infection is getting worse."

"I know, honey. I miss them too. I also wish I were here every night. This project won't end until August. And I'll be gone Monday through Thursday every week. This client is very important to the firm and they're counting on me to demonstrate leadership."

"I know...I know. I don't want to talk about it anymore. It just upsets me," Olivia finally said.

Alex went to bed that night wondering if he was pursuing the right things in life. His current job paid him handsomely and allowed for Olivia to be able to stay home with the kids. But every Monday morning when he left for the airport it was becoming more and more painful to say good-bye to his children. He often felt guilty, especially when little Lindsay would cry. When he came home on Thursday evenings, he was physically and mentally exhausted. He began to truly treasure his weekends and refused to open his laptop or check any voice mails over the weekend. He would spend every moment of the weekends with his wife and children.

Alex was working on a major account in Dallas and his project manager, Paul Grimes, was up for promotion to partner and was under a good bit of pressure to deliver a successful project. The project manager, in turn, transferred that pressure onto the team. This made for a not-so-wonderful working environment.

Alex decided he would talk to the head of his office in Atlanta, his managing partner Gary Harrington. He would do it on Friday when he returned from Dallas.

Alex arrived at the Dallas airport Monday morning and it took him over an hour to get a rental car. He promised himself, as he did every week, that he would call the airport and offer to reengineer their car-rental process for free. It made no sense for all the people to board one bus, the same bus from where people were also disembarking, and to go to one terminal for all car rentals.

He arrived at his project site in Plano and was immediately called to a meeting with Paul Grimes. Paul said he had just been informed that the client's executive leadership wanted a major update on Friday morning and that Alex was going to be responsible for it. Alex usually returned home on Thursday nights and it was an expectation both he and his family demanded of his travels.

What would you do at this point if you were in Alex's shoes?

Before Alex could respond, Paul's phone rang and the meeting was over.

Alex was upset that Paul did not push for a Thursday meeting, but decided that since this was an exception, he would indeed fly home after the presentation on Friday.

If you were Alex, how much of your $100 of emotional energy do you think has been spent already?

"Hey Alex, did you hear about King Hussein dying in Jordan? Gene Siskel dies last week, Joe DiMaggio dies, George Clooney leaves ER and oh, the Knicks picked up Latrell Sprewell—what's this world coming to?" said Jack.

Jack was on Alex's team and always had the CNN home page up on his laptop.

"Not today, Jack. Not today," Alex said quietly.

"What?" Jack inquired.

"It's Monday! Can you just do your damn job?" Alex yelled.

How many emotional dollars did Alex just lose here and how much did he just take away from Jack?

_____

_____

_____

How much responsibility did Alex have to replete his emotional energy after his meeting with Paul and before engaging with anyone else? What could Alex have done differently?

_____

_____

_____

How possible is it for you or any human being to discard emotionally draining experiences (bricks), compartmentalize them and still be emotionally healthy?

_____

_____

_____

_____

Alex was not coping well with his unplanned additional workload and was looking forward to the Wednesday afternoon phone call with Gabe, Briana, and sometimes, Iseus. This was their week to call and talk to each other. He really began to enjoy the conference calls and eagerly anticipated them. He wondered how Briana and Gabe were doing.

Gabe had moved in with a friend from work, Jim. He was single and did not mind having a rising star of the company stay with him.

Gabe left home that infamous night. He returned the next day during lunch to pack up most of his belongings, leaving Heather a venomous note warning her not to call him—that he would call he when he was ready. She had tried to call him several times anyway, but he had been too hurt, angry, and confused to acknowledge her calls. He spoke to her briefly last week and they agreed to meet tonight at The Pewter Rose, a quiet restaurant in town. He had not the faintest notion of what he was going to say. This only exacerbated his anxiety.

Jim, Iseus, Alex, and Briana were the only people Gabe had shared his ordeal with. He wondered about what his friends would think of him— they all looked up to him and thought of him as having the perfect life: a young rising talent within the company with a beautiful wife who let him do whatever he wanted. Would they think less of him? Would his boss, Joe Brathway, think less of him? He could always tell them it was her fault. After all, she cheated on him. But Gabe knew he was to blame. He was consumed with a deep sense of failure. He had failed himself. He was no different from his father and that realization bothered him immensely. What would his father think? Gabe had always taken liberties in exaggerating how much better of a man and husband he was. What had he done? His loose bricks were destroying him. Why was life continuing to punish him so much? Why could he not be normal like everyone else? These questions had been eating away at Gabe for many weeks now.

Suffice it to say, he channeled all his energy into his work. He began to work 14-16 hour days and made sure every "t" was crossed and every "i" was dotted on all the projects in his department. He would fight back, he thought. He conceded defeat to life and to his marriage, but he would be damned if he would fail at something he controlled. He became more reclusive and disguised his anguish quite well from the people in his department. He made Jim swear not to tell anyone what was going on.

Which one of Gabe's loose bricks is coming into play here?

_____
_____

_____

Gabe took comfort in knowing he was going to talk to Alex and Briana before having dinner with Heather. He could solicit their counsel, he thought.

How do you think Gabe is reacting to this experience? How would you react if you were in his shoes?

_____
_____

_____

How do you typically react to high stress times?

_____
_____

_____

What are some of the specific stress relieving activities you do?

_____
_____

_____

Briana had just left Gabe and Alex an urgent e-mail saying that she had asked Iseus to join them in their conference call.

Briana had been going through some changes at work, but nothing of any significant nature. She had moved into a remodeled office and was quite excited about having the proverbial corner office. She had spent most of yesterday preparing for her annual goal-setting session with her boss, Michael Skinner. Michael liked her and wanted her to be successful. Although he was her advocate, he was very ineffective as her counselor. He rarely gave her constructive feedback on anything and approached the performance review process with little preparation.

When she arrived at Michael's office he was on the phone. She waited outside. And waited. The appointment was for 10AM and it was now 10:30! Briana had amassed a great deal of anxiety.

How many emotional dollars (and why) do you think Briana spent waiting for Michael?

_____

_____

_____

How often do you hold your meetings on time? How can you prevent the depletion of emotional dollars of employees that have scheduled meetings with you?

_____

_____

_____

Finally at about 10:40AM, Michael yelled, "Briana! Come in. Come in! Sorry about that—old college buddy of mine just in town this week."

How much more of that daily $100 did Briana burn after hearing Michael's excuse?

_____

_____

_____

What would you do at this point if you were Briana?

_____

_____

_____

"Oh, that's okay—better late than never," Briana said.

"So, annual goals, hey? I take it you've already put something together?" Michael asked.

Briana knew she was fully depleted with his last question, and she realized that this was going to be another unproductive session—one of the many in the last five years.

Which one of Briana's loose bricks is coming into play here?

_____

_____

_____

Briana gave Michael Skinner her goals sheet. She listed the following goals for the next fiscal year:
- Develop a better master scheduling structure for the hospital
- Provide the nurses with more unconventional continuing education courses
- Merge with two of the other wings and wards of the hospital and leverage vendor contracts
- Continue through December with the Leadership Session begun in Atlanta
- Spend more time developing skills for Senior Hospital Administrator

"I'm going to put together a year-long action plan for each one of those goals and be very disciplined about following them, Michael."

"Well, where do I sign this form now?" he responded.

"At the bottom of the last page there."

"Okey-doke! Super—let me know if I can do anything," Michael Skinner concluded.

"Thanks," Briana mused.

And with that Briana stormed out of his office and went straight to the phone and called one of her best girlfriends.

In a goal-setting session like this, how could you be more prepared?

———————————————————
———————————————————
———————————————————

What would you do to engage Michael Skinner?

———————————————————
———————————————————
———————————————————

Briana felt better after talking on the phone. She decided she would go outside, have lunch and read the cartoons (it was her favorite section). This was her way of playing out her meeting with Michael Skinner as well as getting in a better mood for the conference call.

"Hello! This is Gabe on the line. Anyone else on yet?"

"Yup! Alex and Iseus are on the line too. How you doing, Gabe?" Briana asked.

"Oh not so good. I finally spoke to Heather last week and we're having dinner tonight. I honestly don't know what I'm going to say. I don't even know if I should ask for a divorce. I'm really confused. Any advice, anyone?"

What advice would you give Gabe?

———————————————————
———————————————————
———————————————————

"I'm the only woman here so I'll give you my perspective, Gabe," Briana blurted out. "Ask yourself if you love her. Do you?"

"I think so. But it will be hard for me to forget what I saw and to forgive her."

"Then tell her just that! But if you love her, Gabe, you gotta try and make things work. You've been married six years and that's a long time. Just talk to her—ask her what she wants." Briana said.

"I never thought this would be happening to me. Alex, Iseus—what do you think?"

"I agree with Briana, bud. You've got to face her. It's been, what, seven, eight weeks?" Alex asked.

"I agree," Iseus said very quietly.

"Talk to me Iseus. Tell me something about life. You always have these great thoughts," Gabe begged.

Iseus obliged after asking Briana and Alex if he could talk for about 10 minutes. He began to talk about the Emotional Theory of Relativity (ETR). He compared it to Einstein's Theory of Relativity—which was based on two objects in motion. Einstein argued that if one were standing on a moving train while watching another train traveling at the same speed right next to it then it would appear, from those two vantage points, that they were both stationary. **One's sense of motion was predicated on what else was in motion.**

"The ETR is similar," Iseus continued. "We gauge our level of happiness or sadness based on some Anchoring Model. **Your happiness today is based in good part on how happy you were yesterday.** Replenishing your emotional dollars when you only have $10 has a significantly different sense of joy than replenishing when you have $90. To have a context for your responses to daily stimuli is only going to help you know yourself better. **To understand yourself today, ask yourself what happened yesterday and what you're hoping for tomorrow.**"

Iseus asked the three to imagine that they had just slightly cut one of their fingers and to think of the ensuing pain. Then he suggested they imagine that sometime afterward they broke one of their arms and to think of that pain.

"Compare the two levels of pain," he instructed.

The group agreed that breaking one's arm was more painful. He then asked them to reverse the sequence of experiences (bricks). That is, to imagine breaking one's arm first and then, at some later point, slightly cutting one's fingers. In this case, he argued, the pain of the cut finger would be significantly lessened because of a more traumatic Anchoring Model of pain—breaking one's arm. This was the relativity of emotion.

Similarly, he said that if everyone on this day were getting a divorce, Gabe would feel better about himself than he does because, relatively speaking, everyone else was going through the same thing. So Gabe could conclude that he is no different than anyone else and, more importantly, no worse than anyone else.

"Remember what I said in Atlanta—there is nothing more threatening to a leader than not understanding yourself. The most important part of the ETR is to find out what your Anchoring Model is. What is the speed of the other train that is making you feel like you are slower or faster? **Who represents that model and is saying to you that what you are feeling is good or bad?**" Iseus asked rhetorically.

"Gabe, are you sad because you are breaking the model of happiness that the world has set for you, or are you sad because you might now have to live life without a companion, which may mean you might not have children any time soon—which I know is important to you?" Iseus asked.

There was a long pause.

"Part of me doesn't feel anything," Gabe finally said. "I feel I can still function quite productively and I know this doesn't sound right, but I neglected Heather because I never really needed her for anything. I guess I got married because it was the thing to do and a definition of success that has always been in my mind. Gosh—I can't believe I just said that. I'm not being fair to her. I'm too selfish and need to figure myself out before I even try to repair this relationship. I think my experiences, the bricks laid in Africa and with my father, were like breaking the arm—and this one is like the finger. Sounds awful, but it's true. **My Anchoring Models are those**

people I work with—how utterly pathetic is that? They are my mirror. I've got to get out of this revolving door. I think I know what to do now. Thanks—all of you."

What/who are your Anchoring Models for success?

_____

_____

_____

Review your loose bricks again on page 47 (you may want to look at your hut) and see if you can pull out what your Anchoring Models in those experiences were.

Loose Brick 1   *Anchoring Model*

_____   _____

_____   _____

_____   _____

Loose Brick 2   *Anchoring Model*

_____   _____

_____   _____

_____   _____

Loose Brick 3   *Anchoring Model*

_____   _____

_____   _____

_____   _____

"Alex, what's up with you?" Briana asked.

"This project in Dallas is taking its toll on me. I have to stay over tomorrow (Thursday) night for a Friday morning presentation with the clients here. John's got a serious ear infection that's been getting worse all week. The whole work-life thing is just wearing me out."

"Can you delegate the presentation and head home?" Gabe asked.

"I wish. But this client is very demanding and the project manager here is walking on ice, so he wants everything to go off smoothly. The client's leadership is getting worried that people in their company are not on board with what we're doing. They're getting a good bit of feedback from people outside the project."

"Resistance Creep!" Iseus blurted out.

"What?" Alex asked.

"**Resistance Creep…the notion during the life of a project that employees are going to hate what's coming and so begin to resist the impending change.** In change management parlance, it is a term we use quite frequently."

"Interesting. Kinda like scope creep, I guess. Well, I'm gonna talk to the head of my office, Gary Harrington, Friday afternoon and figure out what my options are. Briana—how about you?" Alex replied.

"I had my annual review session with my boss and he so does not care. It lasted five minutes! I don't have a choice. I'm stuck with him and I really have to fend for myself. I don't know what else to do."

"Can this guy sabotage anything you're working on? I mean if you go and achieve your goals, could he get upset at how you achieve them?" Gabe asked.

"I'm not sure I understand your question, Gabe," Briana asked.

"Well, you may just want to keep him posted on a regular basis on what's going on and how you are progressing towards your goal. That way you won't get any of that 'Resistant Creep' from him!" Gabe clarified.

Everyone started laughing—**Resistance Creep was an amusing way of labeling lack of support, but somewhat appropriate.**

What kind of Resistance Creep do you experience in your project work?

_____

_____

How does Resistance Creep typically go away at your workplace?

_____

_____

_____

What have been some of the implications of Resistance Creep not being mitigated at your workplace?

_____

_____

_____

The conference call lasted about an hour and a half. Everyone wished both Gabe and Alex luck with their challenging next couple of days.

A few hours after the conference call, as Gabe was getting ready for his dinner with Heather, Alex's mobile phone rang. It was Olivia.

"Honey, I've had to take John to the hospital. It's not serious but they are going to keep him overnight. Any chance you can come home tonight?" Olivia asked.

"Olivia, I can't. In fact, I have to stay over tomorrow night as well."

"Listen, I'm sick of this. Your son is in the damn hospital. If you give a damn about your family, you'll be home!" Olivia screamed and hung up.

If you were Alex, what would you do now?

_____

_____

_____

Alex was upset. He thought about his dilemma and went to see Paul immediately.

"Paul, my son's in the hospital. The presentation is all done—Jack is printing out the final version now. I've got to go home tonight—it's my family," Alex said rather hastily.

"Alex, this is very important, too. You can go, but just know that this is a data point for me," Paul threatened.

Alex was furious at Paul's insinuation, but was convinced he made the right decision. He said nothing, however. He walked away, packed, raced to the airport and got home by 11PM.

Gabe arrived at The Pewter Rose and sat in his car for a few minutes taking deep breaths. He knew this was not going to be easy.

He walked upstairs to the restaurant and saw that Heather was waiting at the bar. How awkward it felt for both of them. Gabe felt strange, as though he were on a blind date.

"Hey," Gabe greeted Heather.

Her eyes were red. He knew she had been crying. She looked great as always. She was still wearing her work suit. Strangely enough, he looked at her as a woman. He looked at her curves and how her skirt accented her long legs. He noticed her hair and thought that he had never really noticed her hair before. He took a deep breath through his nose, knowing that this might be the last time he would smell that perfume coming from her body. She looked good, he thought. How could he have not noticed before?

Gabe felt himself becoming transformed. A serene sense of calmness coddled him. He looked around and could neither see nor hear anything in particular. He looked back at Heather and smiled. He was at peace. He was going to do something right. He was going to lay a strong brick. This was not going to cost him any emotional money.

"You OK?" Heather asked.

"Yes, let's get seated."

Neither looked at the menu. They just stared at each other. They both seemed surprised that the other was calm and appeared unmoved at what they were about to do. They seemed to know. How could this be?

"Gabe, it's been over for a long time. I just never had the courage to tell you. I feel relieved. I feel relieved I don't have to lie to you anymore. I feel relieved I can be honest with you. And I feel relieved because I think I am giving you what you really want—time for yourself," Heather said with a calm but cracking voice.

"I want to apologize to you, Heather. I am sorry for stealing these last few years of your life. I always told myself after Africa that I would never be unhappy or cause anyone to be unhappy. Please know that I did not intentionally ignore you all those years—I guess I really didn't know how to live with someone who had her own needs and ambition and life. I hope you can give me a second chance, Heather," Gabe pleaded.

"I truly can't. I am in love with another man. He makes me happy and I want to be with him. I tried to make things work for us for so long—I got exhausted doing it by myself. Gabe, I pray that you will grant me what I truly want for you to experience in your life before you die—I want you to be able to love and be loved by someone; so you can see the world as a beautiful place to live instead of a place of battle where you have to rush to win all the time," Heather said calmly.

Tears began rolling down Gabe's cheeks. He was not angry with Heather. **He was angry that life was teaching him an important lesson at such a high price.**

Heather got up, leaned over to Gabe, kissed his forehead gently, and walked out of the restaurant with tears of her own.

"The only cure for sadness is to learn something."

—*T. H. White*

Chapter Six

MORTALITY FOR MANAGERS
SUMMER, 1999

THE FOLLOWING IS TAKEN FROM A NEPALESE GOOD LUCK MANTRA

1. Take into account that great love and great achievements involve great risk. Judge your success by what you had to give up in order to get it.

2. When you lose, don't lose the lesson.

3. Learn the rules so you know how to break them properly.

4. When you realize you've made a mistake, take immediate steps to correct it.

5. Spend some time alone.

6. Open your arms to change, but don't let go of your values.

7. A loving atmosphere in your home is the foundation for your life. Do all you can to create a tranquil, harmonious home.

8. In disagreements with loved ones, deal only with the current situation. Don't bring up the past. And don't let a little dispute get in the way of a great friendship.

9. Share your knowledge. It's a way to achieve immortality.

10. Once a year, go some place you've never been before.

Author unknow
Source: Internet

It was the last summer of the 21ˢᵗ Century. Tae Bo was the new health craze everyone was talking about. Susan Lucci finally won her Emmy (her 18th try), and 'Star Wars—The Phantom Menace' opened in grand fashion at the box office along with 'Austin Powers—The Spy Who Shagged Me'. While the 'Blair Witch Project' kept everyone away from the woods, 'The Sixth Sense' was keeping everyone from sleeping. The San Antonio Spurs won the shortened NBA season. There were national tragedies also. James Byrd Jr., a black man in Texas, was dragged to his death and Billy Jack, a gay man, was killed in Alabama. The most traumatic event was the massacre at Columbine High School in Littleton, Colorado. Parents and children around the country lost their innocence that day.

What are some other events of this summer that mattered to you?

_____

_____

_____

In middle management America, Alex, Gabe, and Briana were all still at their respective jobs. Gabe and Heather officially filed for divorce. North Carolina required them to be legally separated for a year before it could be finalized. In the legal process, Gabe and Heather fought over absolutely nothing—they disposed of all their assets equally and amiably. It was apparent they cared for each other. Heather moved out and gave the golf community house back to Gabe. Gabe made an official announcement to his department during a staff meeting about his pending divorce, and encouraged mutual friends to regard Heather as they normally would. He never spoke of that night again.

Alex was not able to connect with the head of his office, Gary Harrington, until today. Gary was a highly respected and well-liked partner of the firm. He was only 43, but his peers and staff marveled at his fairness, his ability to make astute decisions, and the way he led by example. He allowed for a good bit of empowerment with the over 800 people he managed in the Atlanta office and was approachable to all.

"Hey Alex," Gary said with his usual smile, "How are things in Dallas?"

Alex always wondered how Gary always knew where each of the 800 people he managed were and what project they were working on.

"Dallas is fine, Gary. How are you?" Alex had to get the formalities out of the way.

"Sorry we haven't been able to connect. What can I do for you?" Gary asked.

Again, Alex was impressed with Gary's genuine desire to help all his employees. He realized right then and there that Gary was his role model—he was the leader Alex wanted to be like.

Who is your leadership model at your company? List the qualities in him/her that you admire.

_____

_____

_____

"Gary, I am wrestling with my travel back and forth from Dallas. It's taking its toll on me and the kids…"

"Lindsay, John, and Taylor," Gary interrupted.

"Yes. Thanks for remembering their names. I'll be honest with you—what are my options here? I mean, I love this firm but I know we travel all the time. I know if I want to make partner, I must demonstrate my commitment here. I truly love this practice and want to stay—I just don't know what to do."

"First, you're not going anywhere. Let's see if we can make things work here. You are one of the best consultants we have and I won't lose you because you have three young children. These are the values I want to see in all the people here."

Alex was moved by Gary's brief but impactful response. He felt humbled by the generosity of a man of Gary's stature. He took a difficult situation and immediately turned it into a challenge.

"Gary, why do you think most people at my level, the managers, leave stable firms like Impact Consulting?"

Gary offered three reasons.

1.   They leave because they realize they cannot possibly rise to the expectations of the higher levels and fill in the shoes of the next level.

2   They leave because they want a lifestyle change—they either want to spend more time with their families or they just want more out of life.

3   Finally, they leave because they are young enough and confident enough to try and do more with their professional lives, like going to a dot com.

What are the reasons you would leave your company?

_____

_____

_____

"Very few leave because I don't pay them well. I will say this though, Alex, **most people who leave for the first two reasons usually end up doing something far less challenging and more monotonous.**"

When your peers leave your company, how successful do they become?

_____

_____

_____

"I would say I fit into the second reason. So what are my options?" asked Alex.

"Well, let's see if we can find you some work in town in the short term at least. Then, I would recommend aggressively partnering with anyone selling work in town and create your own destiny here. I will support you if I see you trying to make things happen as well."

Gary was being more than generous with this offer. Alex accepted the challenge.

Alex wanted to take advantage of the opportunity and probe Gary more on his leadership style.

"Gary, if you have a few more minutes, I want to ask you about another issue I have been thinking about recently—leadership. Out of curiosity, who did you model your leadership style after?"

Gary explained that he could not personally tolerate having a boss and reporting to one. Because of this, he decided his style would be to never boss anyone else. He understood the need for hierarchy in any organization, but it was more of a necessary evil than anything else. Someone had to sign the paychecks and determine raises, promotions, and strategy. He said he was very much a value-centered leader and believed in trusting his partners and staff to do the right thing. He said Impact Consulting was made up of smart people and his job was to keep peace in the family so they could all harness the collective power of each other.

"You know, Alex, I hope that leadership is an evolutionary concept—a continuous work-in-progress. The great ones, like Jack Welch at GE, adapt to the needs of the times and the changing faces of their workforce. **I would argue that there is still room for the savior or the hero in most organizations, but he or she is replaceable by someone versatile and adaptable.** If you want longevity as well as to leave a legacy, you must adopt an adaptable leadership style.

Forgive me for rambling, Alex, but I've been thinking about this lately too. I would say that the leadership model of the future has to be one of interdependency. I mean, **the leader has to figure out how to take multiple** perspectives because, let's face it, none of us knows what the heck we're doing, and bring them together in a manner that everyone sees as beneficial to the overall output of the company."

What are the professional values and virtues that you adhere to?

_____

_____

_____

Review your hut. (page 30)

What is your current leadership style?

_____

_____

_____

What would you like your leadership style to be?

_____

_____

_____

How will you fill the gap between the two questions above?

_____

_____

_____

Who can help you fill the gap?

_____

_____

_____

How can your values and desired leadership style help you make decisions and prioritize?

_____

_____

_____

"Okay, since I have you going, Gary, what qualities do you look for in a manager that you consider to be good leadership qualities?" Alex probed even further.

Gary submitted the following list to Alex:

1. Character
2. Managers must have a thought out leadership style. They can adapt it from someone they know or could have read about one
3. Cheerleader
4. Managers must have the ability to move a group of people toward a desired goal that adds value to the company and its customers
5. Passion
6. Value-centered approach to everything they do. The age of command and control is losing its place in the world
7. Sincerity
8. Ability to be interdependent even if it is not reciprocated
9. Follow through to completion
10. Good leaders are constant followers themselves—they find roles where they can follow someone else and support him/her in the company

List additional qualities you think should be included.

_____

_____

_____

"Gary, I have to be honest. I see lists like these in every management book I read. People have these trite lists. Why is it still difficult to follow any of them consistently?"

"Well, you asked me for mine and I answered off the top of my head. But aside from that, I think managers have fewer living role models and companions than I used to. Leaders are so caught up in the chase for the new big deal that months and sometimes years go by and they have not done any succession planning. They have not passed down what was passed to them. Many leaders think that once they become leaders, their days of following are over. This couldn't be farther from the truth. Most of this isn't brain surgery, it's just someone spending time teaching managers what is expected of them from their company and how to meet those expectations.

Another thing with all these grandiose lists is that no one tells you how to have character, how to be sincere, or how to follow through. The 'how to' is the hard part. **Someone once told me that the difference between greatness and potential greatness is in completion. The 'how to' is to get up and do something that has a significant chance of failure.** And, regardless of the outcome, you will build character. **You are only going to learn to be sincere by volunteering in your community and giving of yourself so that no one but you knows what you have done. If you want passion, do things you aren't expected to do but that you believe in. You haven't done anything until you've changed someone's mind. You haven't done anything until you've made something better because of an idea you had that was met with resistance.** You must appreciate your time by appreciating your mortality—many of you think you'll be at this age for the rest of your lives. You will grow old."

What sounded like a long lecture was a passionate conversation with Gary. Alex was firmly convinced he was in the presence of his role model.

"Let me do a little exercise with you, Alex," Gary said, almost as Alex was about to get up and leave. "Let me ask you three questions."

"Fire away, Gary."

"These questions are not religious questions—they are philosophical questions, okay? The first one is: Would you feel good about a confrontation with Satan?"

Answer this question for yourself.

_____

_____

_____

Alex thought about the very strange and somewhat uncomfortable question. Then he responded, "Yes. I think he would be someone I would be proud to disagree with."

"Okay, the second question is—how would you feel good about confronting someone that exhibited unethical or unacceptable behavior?"

Answer this question for yourself.

_____

_____

_____

Alex thought this question was easier than the first one. "Of course. I would have no problems doing that!"

"Finally, Alex, would you feel good about confronting someone that exhibited unethical or unacceptable behavior if that someone was your boss?"

Answer this question for yourself.

_____

_____

_____

Alex wrestled with this last question. After a few moments, he replied, "I am not sure. I would if the behavior was detrimental or abusive. In all honesty, if it were something I could ignore, I would probably ignore it. My boss could impact the rest of my family and that price is too high. It's a difficult situation."

Which of your professional values and virtues do you consider non-negotiable and why?

_____

_____

_____

"I was once told that learning was a great habit, but thinking was an even better one. So, let me leave you with this thought until we meet again: Did I just ask you three identical questions?"

Alex was indeed puzzled.

"Alex, the line between being insane and being a genius is very thin—dare yourself to walk there sometime," Gary concluded.

With that, Gary stood up and told Alex he would get back with him soon on his original request.

What do you think about Gary's parting thought?

_____

_____

_____

Alex felt as if he had just had a conversation with Iseus and was eager to get to the conference call later on in the day to ask Iseus what he thought about Gary's questions.

As Alex walked away, he remembered the pledge he had made himself in January about confronting his seemingly non-existent loose bricks.

He went into his office and shut the door. Gary was right, he thought, and it was time to face himself. They were indeed three identical questions.

Alex began to think about why he was risk averse and conflict averse. He rarely went to battle for anything. This was different from choosing one's battles—he was avoiding them all.

As much as he cherished his childhood, he dreaded that his Anchor Model was to always stay clear of anything that was not associated with school for his kids, church, and family. These three were great surrogate institutions of learning, but he never engaged in anything that truly opened his eyes to the tragedy and chaos of the world around him. **As a child, he was told it was not his world.**

But it was his world. And he had a responsibility, he agreed, to all of it. He decided to make two immediate changes:

1. Take more chances
2. Expose his children to the diversity of life in Atlanta by getting them engaged in challenging and mind-opening programs

What are some risks/challenges you would like to take in the next year?

_____

_____

_____

At about the same time that Alex was concluding his session with himself, Briana was getting ready to have a challenging performance session with one of the nurses. The nurse, Jill Brown, had been repeatedly tardy and Briana had avoided addressing the several complaining voicemails she had received from the other nurses. But she knew she could no longer put off the confrontation. It was time to give difficult feedback to one of her good nurses.

Jill walked into Briana's office and immediately said, "Well, it must be nice to have us all do the work so you can have such a large office."

How would you respond to this comment?

_____

_____

_____

"Come in, Jill. Would you mind shutting the door, please? Thank you. Tell me what's going on with you, Jill."

"Why? What are you hearing?"

"I'm hearing you're late a good bit these last few weeks, and I was certain something must be going on with you because you're usually on time."

Critique Briana's role thus far. What would you do differently?

_____

_____

_____

Jill was agitated and moved restlessly in her chair. She was obviously uncomfortable with what was taking place.

"My personal life is my business, not this hospital's! Besides, I've only been late a few times. Who has been complaining?"

"Jill, you know I can't give you names. And I know it's your business and what you do outside of these walls is no one's business but yours. But what you do here is our business. Jill, we deal with patients…"

"I know who we deal with! Are you trying to insult me?"

Make a note of why giving difficult feedback to employees might be challenging for you.

_____

_____

_____

"No, Jill. Not at all. I am just trying to understand why you have been late 11 times in the last month? I know you've only been with us for about six months, but I have a responsibility to maintain a schedule here and everyone has to play their part. I have to write you up, Jill, whether you tell me or not. If you tell me, maybe I can help and reschedule you for more convenient times. Please, work with me here."

Again, critique Briana's handling of the feedback session.

_____

_____

_____

Jill looked down at her shoes. She was subdued by the calmness of Briana's comments. She then proceeded to tell Briana about her sick mother who had moved in with her. Caring for her, Jill said, was the most challenging experience of her life. She had been forced to give up everything she did outside of her job to accommodate her mother. It had been a trying time for her.

Briana crumpled up the Feedback Form and told Jill of the Adult Care wing in the hospital and the Employee Assistance Program that allowed employees of the hospital to bring adults to the center, like day care for children. Briana promised Jill she would help her get her mom in if she promised to never be late again. They continued talking about their families and learned that they were the same age with parents of similar ages as well.

"Thank you," Jill said as she walked out of Briana's office.

What are your thoughts on the resolution Briana reached? Would you have done anything differently?

_____

_____

_____

Look at the list you created on page 88 (reasons why giving difficult feed-back is challenging for you). What can you do to adequately prepare and replete your emotional energy before such sessions?

_____

_____

_____

List three major conflicts you have had in the last five years. Who were they with and what were they about? How did you resolve them?

Conflict #1

_____

_____

_____

Conflict #2

_____

_____

_____

Conflict #3

_____

_____

_____

Briana turned her chair to the window and looked out at nothing in particular. What had started off as almost a certain $100 worth of emotional depletion ended up with a burst of energy. The experience, this brick, reminded Briana of the reason she loved her job. She was a problem solver and added value to the hospital and its patients by solving problems for doctors, nurses, and staff. She felt proud. She was anxious to get on the phone and tell Iseus, Gabe, and Alex who, by now, had become special friends.

It was 2PM.

"Hi gang! Sorry I'm late," Briana blurted out once she dialed into the conference call.

"Have you heard?" Alex asked.

"Heard what? What's up? Alex, are you having another kid?"

"No! JFK Jr.'s plane crashed. He and Carolyn Bissette and Carolyn's sister were all killed. He was flying his small plane and crashed on his way to his cousin's wedding. Can you believe that?"

"Oh no! I liked John John. Are you sure? Boy, that family is just cursed with bad luck and he was the best one of those Kennedys. I'm in shock. We are about the same age, you know?" Briana responded in disbelief.

"I know. I was just thinking about how great it would be if he had become president. How tragic," Gabe said solemnly.

"I tell you, this is shocking. I remember my dad telling me that one of his most vivid memories was the death of JFK in Dallas. He says he remembers exactly where he was and who he was with and what he was doing," Alex slowly added.

What are some of the more vivid memories of your life?

_____

_____

_____

_____

_____

Iseus felt the tone of the conversation shift to a somber one. He wanted to talk about mortality because it was subject matter he was supposed to cover before the end of the year with the three. He did not know whether this was the right time. But his intuition told him that it might be. Some of his previous sessions on mortality did not go as well as he would have liked. He knew it was because one's frame of mind had to be wrestling with this concept for any learning of substance to occur. He decided he would ask.

"I'm supposed to cover the concept of leadership and your mortality with you all in the fall. Our research tells us that one of the phenomena that great leaders need to become intimate with is their mortality. Do you all want to talk about this now?"

To Iseus' surprise, they all responded in the affirmative. It was quiet.

"I am going to ask you all some difficult questions. Take your time and respond to them as honestly as you can. Okay?"

Gabe and Briana acknowledged their readiness. Alex remembered his conversation with Gary and his two subsequent self-indulgent declarations. He wondered if life was attempting to send him a signal that he might have made the right ones. He would learn, he decided. Nothing bad ever came from genuinely trying to better oneself.

"There are three questions and no right or wrong answers. This is not a trick question, I assure you. I want you all to write down your responses and after we're done sharing them here, email them to each other."

They were ready.

"If you found out today that you only had six months to live and that by December, when we're all supposed to meet in Miami, you would die, what would you do? Where would you go and whom would you go with? Try to avoid clichés, and answer the questions as realistically as possible. Take a few minutes and let me know."

Answer this question with the same instructions.

_____

_____

_____

A few minutes went by. Finally, Gabe spoke.

"I think I would go back to Africa and visit all the places where I grew up. I left 15 years ago and I have not been back since. I think I would go by myself and just reflect on my life and the journey that life's circumstances have navigated me through."

Alex went next. It was still very quiet.

"I would take Olivia and all my kids, get in a van and just drive across America. To be realistic, I would make sure they were all financially secure first, and then beg my company to let me enjoy six months with my family."

Alex paused. Briana followed.

"I would go see my parents in Mt. Vernon, New York. They are absolutely dear to me and I think I would want to be where I grew up, like you, Gabe, but not alone. And I would just talk about my 38 years on this world with them. What about you, Iseus, you gotta 'fess up too," Briana suggested.

"Okay. I would write. I have seen the world and I would want my thoughts and learnings to be captured somewhere so that others don't have to go through the pain I went through to learn those lessons. I would stay in beautiful La Jolla and go out every night with my wife."

"Amen, brother!" Gabe blurted out.

"Now the second question and the same instructions—be as realistic as possible. Imagine the question to be real. If you found out that you only had one day to live, what would you do, where would you go, and who would you go with? Remember, tomorrow, at this very time, you will die."

Answer this question with the same instructions.

_____

_____

_____

It took longer than a few minutes for the three to respond to Iseus' second question.

Alex went first. "I would call Olivia and tell her to get all the kids and meet me at the airport. I would get on the next flight out and just sit on my deck at home. I would cook the kids hamburgers and watch them eat. I would read to them their favorite stories and kiss them until my lips hurt. I would make love to Olivia one last time and beg her forgiveness for leaving her to raise the kids by herself. I would want all of my family there so I could apologize to everyone. I wish I were only half the man they think I am. I would tell them how much I loved them all and how lucky they were to have next week and the week after. "

Briana began to cry. "Alex, that is beautiful. I envy the love in your life. You are blessed in ways that neither Gabe nor I are. I hope you know how lucky you are to have experienced what you have."

She paused and continued.

"With one day, I would still fly to Mt. Vernon. That is where it all began and that is where I would want it to end. I would ask my mother to cook my favorite meal—the famous six-layered meat lasagna with garlic bread and a Caesar salad with her special homemade vinaigrette dressing. I'd call all my girlfriends and tell them to stop being so picky with men and just take a chance with life! I would want to be in my bedroom tomorrow."

"Well," Gabe started slowly, "I am not sure what I would do. I would call my mother and my brother, but I still would not talk to my dad. Screw him. Life's too short to wait for someone to accept you, you know what I mean? He never did and one day is not going to change that. I would be by myself—I know that sounds pathetic—but I would. I would go to some park and feed the ducks and feel the warmth of the sun. That's where I'd like to be tomorrow afternoon. Iseus?"

"One day? Phew. I do this fairly often and still get choked. I think I would spend half the day making a videotape and just being honest on it. I would ask that the tape be shown at my funeral, like Andy Kaufman did. I would spend the other half of the day with my wife—asking her what she will do with the rest of her life. I would want to die in her arms—outside, like Gabe."

"Alright. Do you all still want to go on with the last question? We'll debrief after that."

Gabe, Alex, and Briana were eager to continue.

"Follow the same instructions with the last question—be as realistic as possible. Imagine the question to be real. If you found out that you only had one hour to live, what would you do, where would you go and whom would you go with? Remember, in about an hour, you will die."

Answer this question with the same instructions.

_____

_____

_____

About ten minutes elapsed before Alex broke the silence.

"Phew! I would call Olivia right away and ask her to round up the kids and put them on speaker phone so I could hear their voices. I would want to hear them all in my last breath. That's it."

Gabe followed, "One hour? I'd find the nearest park and take a few beers with me. I really would. I would go by myself and just enjoy the last hour. I would not call anyone—what would be the point? They were never around for me when I was alive. I would not think about anything or anyone—nothing at all. I'd just soak up the hot rays and enjoy a few cold ones. I'm just being honest, y'all."

There was a pause. Gabe's honesty and vulnerability stunned everyone. But he was telling the truth and that made everyone care about Gabe even more. Briana finally spoke.

"I would stay on this call with anyone that wanted to for about 30 minutes and talk about the world. I would talk about all the things that I did not know, and all the things I did not experience. I love listening to Alex's story about his wife and kids. And I love Iseus' wisdom and I would yell at Gabe for being so stubborn and hardheaded. I would tell him to stop being angry and that if I had all the days he had in front of me, I would start living today. My father gave me the best definition of peace—he said it was the absence of anger. It upsets me that you are so angry, Gabe. I would die proud if, as one of my last acts, I could help you see the world for its beauty.

I would spend the other half hour on the phone with my parents, and I would want their voices to be the last ones I heard, just as they were the first ones I ever heard," Briana said calmly.

Iseus went last, "I'm in my office here at home. I would tell all of you that I have seen great growth and development from you and that I sincerely felt the world would be better because you three were leading it in some capacity. I would ask my wife to come home, she works only a few miles down the road, and I would just lay in her arms and let her tell me how much she would miss me."

"So, Iseus, what was this all about?" Gabe asked after another brief pause.

Iseus first asked everyone how they felt and whether it was depletion or a repletion of emotional energy.

How would you answer this question?

_____

_____

_____

They all agreed that although it was emotionally exhausting, it did not feel like it cost any emotional money. It felt, they said, as though it were a rude awakening of sorts, but one that would be helpful and eventually add emotional money to the rest of their day.

Iseus explained that what they had just revealed to each other was their value system. They had revealed to each other, and to themselves, what part of the world they considered home. Home would be the place of greatest comfort and least threat. They had also revealed what the most important things to them were, who the most important people in their lives were and even their real aspirations. He said they ought not to be surprised if, in a few years, life tricked them and they were in the shoes of the other people on the conference call. He said he could see Gabe becoming Alex and Alex becoming Gabe through some unfortunate set of circumstances.

He told Gabe that a trip to Africa as soon as possible was warranted. He also told him that he began his day not with $100 like everyone else, but with only about $50. He had spent $50 before he even woke up. He told Gabe that he was carrying an enormous burden and agreed with Briana that he needed to figure out how to be at peace and let go of his anger.

But how do I do that, Iseus?" Gabe asked.

"There is no right answer. You have to have faith that going to back to Africa will help give you at least a portion of that answer. But if you think you are a great leader now with only $50 a day, imagine what you would be capable of if you had $100 like everyone else. And don't be fooled, Gabe, in every human being there is a sensory mechanism that tells us whether one is sincerely happy—my guess is that your people follow you for the wrong reasons. Ask them what they like about you as a person and not as a financial genius. See what they come up with. Leadership is about sharing your joy of living and the way your share your skills with the world. It is not about being good at one thing at the expense of all others. Sorry, but I'm just being honest, too."

There was another pause. Then, Gabe's voice cracked over the phone. "Thank you," he said.

What specific advice would you give Gabe?

_____

_____

_____

"Alex, you responded to all the questions almost identically. You have a very firm understanding of your values and what is important to you. Be careful that your career and professional aspirations do not compromise your values. It is a great time to be alive for you, so enjoy it, every minute of it. And there is no reason to not do more of the things you said you'd do if you only had one day. It's your day and it's your life."

Alex thanked Iseus too.

What specific advice would you give Alex?

_____

_____

_____

"Briana, you're in the middle of Gabe and Alex. I don't know if you fully understand what your value system is and whether you're leading the kind of life you truly want to be leading. That's okay though. Not everyone everywhere at all times is supposed to have it all figured out. But there is a void in your heart and you, too, start off each day with about $80. I don't know exactly what it is but I would like to talk to you further and maybe Gabe and Alex can help me figure out what it is that I am feeling."

Gabe and Alex agreed with Iseus and said they would think about it, too.

"Actually, Iseus, there is something on my mind that I want to talk to you about. Are you available to talk tonight because I know we've been on this call for almost two hours now?" Briana asked.

"I will make time," Iseus promised.

"Iseus, you're a change management guy, aren't you? I need help with this project I'm working on. I have Resistance Creep all over the place," blurted Alex as everyone was about to hang up.

"I'll e-mail you a matrix, Alex. Thank you all for your candor. I hope you all saw the value of what we did in your lives and roles as managers."

They all said they thoroughly enjoyed it. **Iseus suggested that they perform this exercise at least once a year with each other.** And he reminded them that no one knew for sure if today would be the beginning of their last six months, last day, or even their last hour.

After the call, Alex called Olivia and asked to speak to the kids. He did not tell her why.

Gabe called his travel agent and asked for some quotes on a trip to Africa.

Briana called her mom and reminisced about her childhood.

"Only a few people are truly awake and they live in a constant state of amazement."

—*Meg Ryan in 'Joe Versus the Volcano'*

Chapter Seven

SINGLES IN MANAGEMENT —THAT NIGHT

Spices for Life

1.   *Think about one miracle every week—envy creativity to the point of being restless about being creative*
2.   *Lend your ears to aged people—they are our forgotten wealth*
3.   *Visit a graveyard—experience true humility at your final destination*
4.   *Stay in and cook a meal—it is the oldest tradition common to all cultures*
5.   *Have lunch in a park all by yourself—we all need time to develop a relationship with ourselves just as we would with someone else*
6.   *Touch someone everyday—hang on to a handshake and a hug a few seconds longer—what better way to feel human*
7.   *Do something for free outside your place of worship, work and residence—test the sincerity of your compassion*
8.   *Make a child laugh—preferably by being goofy—adults need to stop pretending they are perfect*
9.   *Upon your death, what do you want to be most remembered for*
10. *Fill your office walls with pictures and mementos of your life's journey—never forget where you came from or you will spend the rest of your life running away from it*

It was about 8PM Central Time in Chicago when Iseus called Briana at her apartment.

"How's Wrigley Field?" he began.

"Oh, I can't see it from my apartment. It's a couple of blocks away. But I do walk outside the stadium every time Sammy's batting or when McGwire's in town."

"So, how are you doing?" Iseus asked.

"First, thanks for calling."

"I never walk away from the proverbial 'coachable moment'—I knew you had something on your mind. So, how are you?" Iseus asked again.

"Tired as always. I didn't have to teach dance today. But I miss those little girls. I thought a great deal about our conference call today. It put me in a strange frame of mind and I'm still in it."

"What feels strange?"

"I don't know. What we did was very important—I've never thought about my mortality that way. Do great leaders think about that a good deal? Do you? It can be quite draining."

"No! I don't think the purpose was to insinuate that you have to think about your mortality all the time. You're right, that would be draining. It's just a great way of finding out what is important to us at any given time and we need that.

Our research indicates that most people have a day-to-day perspective of only three years—our minds can only actively engage in our thinking process what has happened to us in the last three years and what we want for the next three years," Iseus responded.

Iseus asked Briana to get a piece of paper. He then instructed her to draw a circle with a straight line running through it (see below).

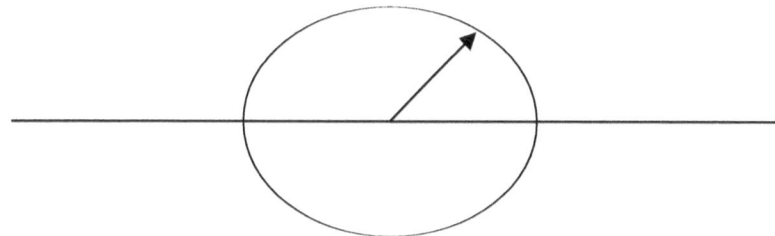

He suggested that if the straight line represented our lifeline, then the circle would represent the three-year frame of mind.

"Most mundane decisions we make are based on that six-year radius which moves towards the right side as we age, assuming life began at the beginning of the line on the far left.

These decisions rarely encompass the breadth of life's experiences, bricks, and the wisdom that collectively and holistically comes from them. By thinking about the matters we have been discussing these past few months in the context of our entire lives, we stretch that circle to form an oval shape resembling an eye (see below). **This allows for infusion of all our bricks—past and future—and that's what you want, especially when you're making difficult decisions.** Does this make sense?" Iseus asked.

The Eye

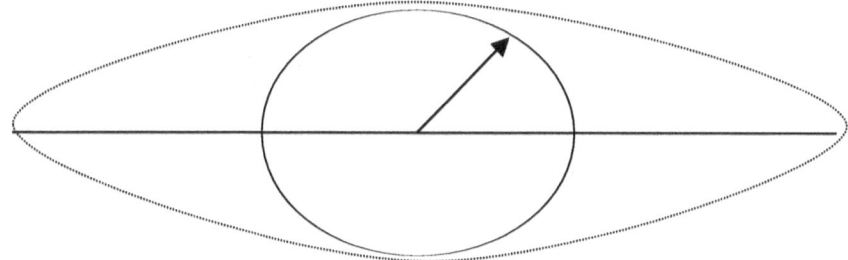

Whom do you consult while making major decisions about your work and personal life?

How would making decisions with the "Eye" perspective help, if at all?

"Yes, Iseus, it makes plenty of sense. I wish I had met you and the guys 10 years ago."

"So what's on your mind?"

"Well, let's take today for example. I had a feedback session with one of the nurses, Jill Brown, and I did not know exactly what to do, so I just got all the facts and did it."

Briana went on to share her experience with Jill. She said she was very proud of the way she handled it and wished she had not left so much to chance. She also wished she could feel like she was not hijacked by circumstance and her insecurities while conducting these sessions.

"You changed the right channels without even knowing it," Iseus said.

"What channels?"

"I promise this will be the last model I'll share with you tonight but it's quite simple and, again, I can't walk away from this teachable moment."

Iseus asked Briana to imagine that in all her direct communications with people, she was employing four channels—he called it the WNTV model (see page 107). The acronym, he said, stood for the four channels which were:

W   N   T   V

Ask yourself—what channel are you going to change?

W—Words—The language you use: The choice of words and phrases

N—Non-verbals—Your body language: What is your face saying? Where are your hands? What is your posture communicating?

T—Tone—What is the tone of your voice implying? How fast or slow are you speaking?

V—Volume—How loud is your voice and how loud does it need to be?

"When you were talking to Jill, you changed the W channel and this is the channel that needs to be changed in direct adult conflict. **Unless you're trying to underscore your changed W, nothing constructive is achieved by changing the NTV channels.** In fact, we have found that an overwhelming number of professionals, especially managers, first change one of the NTV channels. From what you told me, it was Jill who was changing the wrong channels. So next time, think about the four WNTV channels. **Remind yourself during the course of a difficult conversation to always change the W channel.**"

Which channel(s) do you change when dealing in direct conflict?

_____

_____

_____

Why do you think you change these channels?

_____

_____

_____

Review your three bricks on conflict in the previous chapter (page 90) and talk about what channels were changed there and why.

_____

_____

_____

On each of the channels below, how much of $100 of emotional energy during conflict do you think each channel consumes?

W_____
N_____
T_____
V_____

"Gosh, Iseus, that's so helpful. Thank you. Why do I always feel like a child around you? There is so much I don't know and I thought I knew a great deal."

"No problem, it really is my honor. That's my mission in life, to share what I know and hope that you will pass it on. So tell me, what's the **real** reason we're talking tonight?"

Briana was quiet. She wondered how Iseus knew.

"Well. You're very intuitive. Iseus, I'm a happy person. I do my job very well and I have plenty of friends and, gosh knows, I have the best parents in the world—they've been married 61 years. But…I just feel like I'm missing something. I do not feel complete."

"What is missing?" Iseus asked.

"I don't know. I'd like to think it's nothing and it'll go away. But the hardest part of my day is coming home to this empty apartment. I would like to be married so that I can have a life partner and would love to have children of my own. But I don't want to get married for the sake of getting married, like Gabe did. So many of my girlfriends are in unhealthy marriages and believe me, I'd rather be me than them and so would they. I guess I'm fighting between my desire to give myself what I deserve in a life partner and my desire to have a family. I just don't want to feel like I'm compromising my dignity. Alex has both and you do too.

It's difficult to be a single woman today, especially at my age. I always thought that by now I'd have a family. And everyone is baffled including myself, as to why this is not the case. I mean, you've seen me—I'm attractive, aren't I? I've been dancing for the last 25 years—I have a great body! And there are so many mean women out there that have these great husbands—are they bribing them? I have a great job and, by golly, I'm a good person, aren't I?" Briana asked in tears.

Iseus kept quiet.

"The other day, this jerk of a doctor left me a note asking me to call him. He didn't ask me in person. Why does being single at my age give every man a reason to think I'm just dying for a date? That infuriates me, Iseus! I hate that life has me in the 'loser' column because I decided not to compromise when I was 30. Yes—I was engaged! I just knew he wasn't the one. He didn't abuse me in anyway. He was kind—but every little voice in me kept saying, 'Run, Briana, run!' like Forrest Gump! I just didn't love him. I never wanted to be a victim of anything."

What kind of advice would you give Briana?

_____

_____

_____

"Say something Iseus, especially since I've totally embarrassed myself."

"Remember the Emotional Theory of Relativity (ETR)? Think about who your Anchor Model of success is? Who is it?" Iseus asked.

Do you agree that life labels singles like Briana unfairly?

_____

_____

_____

Does your workplace have many singles and does being single impede their careers?

_____

_____

_____

How can being single be advantageous?

_____

_____

_____

"Well, to go back to my loose bricks, I guess it's my parents. I wanted to have what they have. They still really like each other and love each other."

"So, do you think life has labeled you a loser, or that you have labeled yourself a loser?"

"I think it's both."

"Which can you change?" Iseus asked.

Briana was quiet and reflective.

"Briana, the single population in the workforce in America is the fastest growing demographic. There are people like you, men and women, everywhere that are disappointed they have not met their soul mate. **But they are also leading very happy lives. Most of these people, however, are following their passion.** We are so much more resourceful, as human beings, than we give ourselves credit for."

Briana was still quiet and reflective. She knew it was up to her to change what she thought of herself. She knew she had it in her to be happy. She was wrestling with how to feel better about entering her apartment every night. She was thinking.

"Describe your perfect day for me. I mean if tomorrow were the best day of your life, what would it look like?" Iseus asked.

Describe your perfect day in detail

———————————————
———————————————
———————————————
———————————————
———————————————
———————————————

"Well, I would wake up and have Katie and Matt on TV while I read the paper and had my coffee. I would want to feel unhurried. Then, I think I would only spend half the day at work and spend the other day at Girl University…"

"You can't spend half a day at work—let's be realistic," Iseus interrupted.

"Maybe not everyday, but I could arrange it at least twice a week. Then I would teach the little girls dancing all afternoon. I'd probably workout after that and have dinner with some friends or cook for myself. Then, I'd put on some Miles Davis or Ella and read a book with a glass of merlot! That would be a great day!" Briana said, laughing.

"Why can't you do that tomorrow?" Iseus asked.

Briana was thinking again.

"What's keeping you from doing that as many days of the week as possible?" Iseus asked again.

Answer this question for yourself.

_____

_____

_____

"I will!" Briana blurted out. "Tomorrow, I will!"

"Good. Briana, **life is too magnanimous and dynamic for one to assume there is only one way to feel complete.** I concede that being married to the one you love is very rewarding, but I can just hear the joy in your voice when you talk about Girl University and volunteering there. Remember, most of management wants and needs a sense of progress and a sense of contribution. If you need your job for financial reasons only, which is understandable, you will have to find other places to get those two senses. You owe it to yourself.

One last question. What would you change about the last 10 years of your life?"

Answer this question for yourself.

_____

_____

_____

"Well, I would have tried to obtain my Masters. I would also have tried to have more skills than I do now, especially in technology. And I would've learned every aspect of hospital administration instead of just what my job required. But you know, I never really knew how different I was until I got into this business and saw all the other people doing my job—most of them didn't care. It was strictly an 8 to 5 job for them. Why do you ask?"

"You just gave me a set of new goals. **It sounds like you have a great deal of living to do and are very far from the person you want to and can be**," Iseus concluded.

"You're right! I'll do it, Iseus. I promise you I'll do it! Thanks. Thanks for your friendship and for bringing Gabe and Alex into my life—they're both good guys and I'm glad you're my friends."

"Good night and, oh, have a perfect day tomorrow!"

"Good night, Iseus!" Briana said with a smile.

She decided she would indeed have that perfect day tomorrow. Before she went to bed, she left a voicemail for her assistant informing her that she would be in late and would only work half the day.

"The value of an idea lies in using it."

—Thomas Alva Edison

Chapter Eight

THE ETHICS AND POLITICS OF BEING A MANAGER FALL, 1999

An elderly carpenter was ready to retire. He told his employer-contractor of his plans to leave the house-building business and live a more leisurely life enjoying his lovely wife he adored—and his extended family. He would miss the paycheck, but he needed to retire. They could get by.

The contractor was sorry to see his good worker go and asked if he could build just one more house as a personal favor. The carpenter said yes, but in time it was easy to see that his heart was not in his work. He resorted to shoddy workmanship and used inferior materials. It was an unfortunate way to end a dedicated career.

When the carpenter finished his work, the employer came to inspect the house. He handed the front-door key to the carpenter. "This is your house," he said, "my gift to you." The carpenter was shocked! What a shame! If he had only known he was building his own house, he would have done it all so differently.

So it is with us. We build our lives, a day at a time, often putting less than our best into the building. Then with a shock we realize we have to live in the house we have built. If we could do it over, we'd do it much differently. But we cannot go back.

Author: Unknown
Source: Internet

It was fall now. Although Mark McGwire hit 66 home runs, his Cardinals did not make the playoffs. It was the Braves and Yankees in the World Series, with the Yankees sweeping the Southerners to become the team of the decade. Justin Leonard hit a long putt to win the Ryder Cup in dramatic fashion.

The hottest show on television is a game show: 'Who Wants To Be A Millionaire?' Hurricane Floyd hammers eastern North Carolina. There is a devastating earthquake in Turkey and an Egyptian airliner mysteriously crashes just after leaving New York.

Chaos reigned in the Montana household. It was 3PM on a Saturday and Olivia and Alex had a date with another couple to see 'Riverdance'. The show was to start at 8PM and dinner reservations were for 6PM. Both Olivia and Alex had been on the phone for over an hour looking for a babysitter. There were none to be found.

Finally, at about 5:30PM, a friend of a friend of a babysitter called. She could make it and she'd be there in 30 minutes. Yes! Alex thought he would be a few minutes late for dinner but, hey, it's Saturday and no one gets seated on time at a restaurant in Atlanta. It was 6:00PM and no babysitter. 6:15PM—nothing. At 6:30PM, Alex instructed Olivia to write down everything the babysitter needed to know because they would have to rush out as soon as she came. Alex called his friend on his mobile and suggested they go ahead and have dinner without them. Olivia finished making the note and feeding the kids at the same time. It was now 7PM and, finally, a young teenager they had never met appeared on their doorstep.

"I'm Alexis. I'm here to babysit. I, like, got lost. Sorry," she muttered.

"Alexis, we're running a little late. Here are the instructions with our mobile numbers. We'll be back by 11. Thanks for coming on such short notice," Alex said ever so kindly.

With that, they rushed off to the show and sat in their seats at 7:50PM. They were so wound up that they ordered several cocktails to calm themselves down.

Alex was describing the above escapade to his friends in the office when the phone rang. It was Iseus.

"Did you get the Coefficient of Change Matrix I sent you for your project? It's like a litmus test to see if you need any change management help," Iseus explained (see matrix below).

"Yes. I have it right here," Alex responded.

Alex had asked Iseus for help on his project. Alex was implementing a new system for his client. Over 3,000 employees would be impacted, and Alex wanted to know if he needed any change management for his project.

The Coefficient of Change Matrix

Question (circle one)	Somewhat Agree	Agree	Strongly Agree	Your Score
Most of the leadership of this company support this project	1	2	3	
The Project Team is a high-performing team that will deliver a successful project	1	2	3	
The job/role of impacted employees will not change more than 50% from what the current job/role is	1	2	3	
There will be more than adequate training provided for all impacted employees	1	2	3	
Total Score				

"It's quite simple and clinically proven, Alex. Just answer the four questions and tally your score at the bottom. If your Coefficient of Change score is 10 or more, you are fine—no need for change management. If your coefficient is between 5 and 10, then you need some help and should talk to an expert about how to get the right resources to help. If your coefficient is below 5, you need to call the Fire Marshall—you need immediate help," Iseus explained.

Think of a project you have worked on recently and take the above test. Do you agree with the result?

_____

_____

_____

"What exactly does that mean? I mean, what exactly does change management mean? I apologize for the silly question," Alex said.

"It's not a silly question. This is one of the most desired competencies for managers today. **Every project a manager leads will involve working with a group of people, changing something, working with key sponsors of the project, and impacting a segment of the workforce.**"

Iseus explained that, in the old paradigm, if a project was on time and on or under budget, it was considered successful. This is no longer the case. Because the investments made on these projects are so significant, sponsors want to make sure they are getting maximum return on investment (ROI). Since technology is and will continue to be the primary driver of change and efficiencies, a manager must understand that these projects need to be successful in one additional area—**in their acceptance by users. This is the new paradigm of success.** This dimension is more intangible and therefore, less measurable and less demanding of attention. Yet, Iseus argued, it was just as critical to the success of a project as the more tangible dimensions like being on budget or on time.

What has been the definition of success for most of the projects you have worked on in the past?

_____

_____

_____

What is your recommended definition of success for the types of projects you work on?

_____

_____

_____

"My coefficient of change is 7. So I need it. What is 'it' though?" Alex asked again.

"'It' is series of tasks and activities that engage the project team with everyone who needs to be engaged. 'It' is figuring out what will happen to whom when and communicating with that group regularly and sequentially. 'It' is being proactive instead of reactive about anything that might lead to Resistance Creep. 'It' is different for every project. **As a leader, you are more responsible for the 'it' than anything else. 'It' is coming up with tangible solutions to intangible challenges.** And not everyone is good at it."

What does 'it' mean to you?

_____

_____

_____

What type of change management skills would you like to improve on as a manager?

_____

_____

_____

Iseus told Alex the now well-known story of David Curan and Xerox. In 1981, Xerox, which had invested heavily in a failing copier called the 3300, was in financial trouble and suffering a public relations nightmare. Its copiers were considered to be of poor quality. Xerox was forced into

Chapter 11. The then CEO, David Curan, began visiting all his manu-
facturing plants. During his 'town hall' sessions, he asked for questions
and comments.

A factory worker, Frank Enos, asked David why he had not just asked
them how they felt about the 3300. Frank said he could have told David
himself that the copier was poorly designed.

David Curan did not have an answer to that question, but began
changing Xerox so that localized feedback was always considered. In 1989,
Xerox was awarded the coveted Baldridge Quality Award, and to accept
the Award in Washington, DC, David Curan took Frank Enos with him.

"**Change management is about the perspective and power of the
Frank Enos' of every company**," Iseus concluded.

How could change management be of benefit in your project work?

_____

_____

_____

Alex was firmly convinced he needed 'it' and proceeded to negotiate a
change order with his client.

At about the same time in Charlotte, Gabe found himself immersed in
political warfare. Gabe's department was recently awarded a coveted $25
million project that impacted several states. The client, Jeb Rose, was a
private developer. The revenue derived off this project for Gabe's company
was enormous, and if they were successful, Gabe would easily make Vice
President next year. The euphoria was short lived because of concerns over
the magnitude of the project, both in terms of resources to do the work
and the management of a myriad of phases. Several vice presidents at
Charlotte Power and Light had immersed themselves in the project. They
all had seniority over Gabe.

During their first planning meeting, it was apparent that the three VPs
did not like each other. Gabe was in no position to mediate because of his

role as an SMP. Each of the VPs had his own vision; the session quickly turned into a shouting match.

After the meeting, Gabe went to his office to think. He quickly realized that if the project failed, he would be made the scapegoat.

What would your strategy be, if you were Gabe?

_____

_____

_____

Gabe decided on a strategy. He would talk to each one of the VPs individually and get a clear understanding of what each wanted. Then, he would orchestrate a compromise—first by himself and, if that failed, he would seek outside help, perhaps from his boss, Joe Brathway.

Gabe met with VP #1.

"Listen, Gabe, I like you," he said. "The other two VPs are both younger than I am and I'm up for President next year. I think you and I can really work miracles with Jeb. I've known him for years. We've got to work with our own internal contractors and keep the money in the family, you know? It's a big job and we can do it all by ourselves."

"But our internal contractors are all working on other jobs and they're not exactly qualified…" Gabe began to say.

"Oh heck, we'll get them off whatever they're working on. Come on, Gabe, this is big money now—none of those $1 or $2 million jobs you're used to working on. I've done this kinda thing before."

Gabe listened and walked back to his office to think.

What would you do now, if you were Gabe?

_____

_____

_____

VP #1 was thinking bottom-line only, Gabe concluded. His desire to keep all the fees internal, though myopic and self-serving, was understandable. But none of the other department heads, Gabe's peers, would allow for their resources to be transferred even if backfill were promised. The people in his department would not buy it, no matter how motivating Gabe could be. It was a bomb waiting to explode. Gabe decided VP#1's approach was impractical, but he was not the person to tell him that.

Gabe then went to see VP #2.

"Listen Gabe," he said, "Duke Farmer himself, our CEO, has asked me to oversee this account. I know VP #1 wants to keep all this work in-house but he is old school and thinks things work the same as they did 100 years ago when he joined the company. I say we outsource the whole thing—you manage it and your department can do all the engineering—but outsource everything else. We'll get the cheapest labor out there—they're all looking for work. We could make them bid and easily get the lowest bidder. We still come out making millions with very limited liability."

"Has anyone communicated to the other two VPs that Duke Farmer has asked you to lead this?" Gabe asked.

"He announced it at our VP meeting last week. He said the other two would act as advisors and I guess they interpreted that to mean they would be running it just because I was the junior of all three of us."

"Well, what would you like me to do?" Gabe asked.

"Do the engineering and outsource the rest."

As he walked back to his office, Gabe knew that this plan was futile. They would only make money if they got the cheapest contractors. That usually meant that a great deal of micro-management would be required for the contractors and the cost would kill his department. The quality of work with the cheapest contractors was usually disastrous. The contractors would ruin even the best design.

What would you do now if you were Gabe?

_____

_____

_____

Gabe decided he would talk to the third VP and then formulate a plan himself. It was not customary for a SMP department head, like Gabe, to be negotiating between the VPs. He was traditionally responsible for implementing only.

He walked into VP #3's office and asked him what he thought. VP #3 wanted to know what the other two VPs thought first, so Gabe told him.

"I think they're both idiots. Neither of them have spent any time in the field like I have. But I'm too old to get into the middle of this. I don't think we can do this job, Gabe. I really recommend turning it over to the bigger boys downtown because when we screw this up, we lose our reputation. I recommend you think about talking to the other VPs about this."

"Maybe we should all meet and discuss this tomorrow afternoon," Gabe suggested.

"We'll just end up arguing again. We should get Duke Farmer involved—he needs to call this shot, but I don't have a relationship with him. The other two VPs do."

And with that Gabe walked back to his office. He was frustrated. He was a successful department head who was now running around scheduling meetings with VPs who did not want to meet. Any one of them could ruin his career. Gabe did not know what to do with the opposing views and could not exert any influence over the VPs. He was between the proverbial rock and the hard place. Gabe was too embarrassed to tell anyone in his department what was going on.

What would you do now, if you were Gabe?

_____

_____

_____

He decided he had to follow protocol. This job was too important and he had worked too hard to screw it up now. He scheduled a meeting with all three for the next day at 11AM. Gabe sent reminder e-mails, voice mails, and even let each of the VP's assistants know.

He also went to Joe Brathway to get his perspective: "Those three stooges have been running this company down. I can't talk to them. See what happens tomorrow and let me know. But I gotta tell ya, ain't much I can do for you."

With that, Gabe began to put his plan together. He wanted to go into the 11AM meeting with a compromise or an alternative that they could take to Duke Farmer for his meeting with Jeb Rose at the end of the week.

Gabe decided, quite rationally, that he would recommend that they extend the timeline of the project. The client would not be adversely impacted since the many phases of the project were not critically dependent on each other. The extra time, from 18 months to 26 months, would be enough for Gabe to hire and train the right crews, and he could redeploy the same crews on other phases of the project. This would be a great advantage as the redeployed teams would have enough knowledge and lessons learned to make the overall project much more successful. Eureka! Gabe was excited.

Gabe worked all night putting together a presentation that outlined all the advantages and disadvantages of the VPs' plans as well as his own.

Did Gabe make the right decision? Why or why not?

_____

_____

_____

It was 11AM and all three VPs showed up. Gabe shared the three different approaches from all the VPs and then presented his.

"It will never work," VP #1 said. "Duke will never agree to asking a client to extend his timeline—that's like conceding defeat even before the battle has begun. What were you thinking, Gabe?"

"I think we are going to fail. It will be impossible to outsource in the time frame we have and impossible to keep everything in house. And if we give up the job, we lose everything. This is the only way out," Gabe said calmly.

What could Gabe have done differently?

_____

_____

_____

"I think I'll compromise to outsourcing. Let's just do that. I'll tell Duke that and expect you to follow through Gabe," VP #1 directed.

The meeting was over.

What would you do now, if you were Gabe?

_____

_____

_____

This was the end, Gabe thought. He was doomed to fail. Every instinct and every brick of his professional experience told him so. He was now even more confused and did not know what to do. Joe Brathway would be of no help. He thought about calling Alex, Iseus, or Briana, but decided against it.

He decided he had nothing to lose and made an appointment to see Duke Farmer.

What rules of conduct or ethics, if any, is Gabe breaking here?

_____

_____

_____

Gabe concluded with strong conviction that he was going to fail either way. He thought about Heather and how his career had consumed him and made him blind to what was important. His life was important and his opinion was important. If Duke Farmer was a smart man, he would listen to Gabe and appreciate the logic of his thinking, the courage he was displaying and the commitment to the well-being of the company.

Just then the phone rang. It was Duke Farmer.

"Gabe! How are you? You did great work with the Finesan Contract."

"Mr. Farmer. I'm doing fine. I just made an appointment to see you later today," Gabe said rather nervously.

"Yes, I know. I just spoke with the VPs and I concur with their recommendation. I suggest you put together our presentation and accompany me to see Jeb Rose. I want him to know I have my best man on the job."

"But that's what I wanted to talk to you about. I don't think it'll work. I really would like to run an alternative plan by you..."

"I know about the extension you recommended; Jeb will never buy it. I'll see you Friday morning," Duke Farmer said and hung up.

What would you do now if you were Gabe?

_____

_____

_____

What is your personal code of ethics?

_____

_____

_____

What is your company's code of ethics?

_____

_____

_____

What ethical boundaries are non-negotiable for you?

_____

_____

_____

How similar are your responses above to the responses of the three questions Gary Harrington asked Alex on page 85. If they are not similar, explain why.

_____

_____

_____

Gabe did not sleep much. He was confused, angry, disappointed, and lonely. He was surprised at how close and supportive Duke was of his VPs. He trusted them and Gabe could not really blame him for that. He wished he had had a chance to talk to Duke Farmer. He knew that going to him now would offend the VPs and Duke Farmer himself. What was he to do? He would decide in the morning. Gabe thought about his life and how he had always followed the rules to appease his father. He thought about who he wanted his Anchor Model to be. He never took any risks that had significant repercussions. He felt terrible about losing his marriage and finally slept vowing never to make the same mistake twice.

The next morning, Gabe called Jeb Rose's office directly and scheduled a meeting with him in the afternoon. Gabe lied and told Jeb that Duke Farmer had wanted Gabe to socialize some of his plans with him prior to their meeting.

Gabe spent the entire morning preparing as many project plans as possible. That afternoon he met Jeb Rose in his office.

"Mr. Rose, the basis of my visit was a lie. I am here on my own account and without the blessing of my company. However, please know that, ironically enough, I am here in the best interest of both my company and yourself, Sir.

I am asking for 10 minutes of your time for me to explain myself. After that, you can call Duke Farmer yourself and have me fired or you can simply ask me to leave," Gabe said confidently.

He had nothing to lose, he told himself. Using Iseus' Emotional Theory of Relativity, he had already experienced the worst in life and getting fired from Charlotte Power and Light would not break him. He had been wounded much worse by people much smarter than Duke Farmer, Jeb Rose, or the three VPs.

"Okay, young man, you have 10 minutes. I should tell you that Duke and I go way back."

"Thank you," Gabe responded. He proceeded to lay out the various alternatives for serving his account.

Gabe presented his solution and provided plans on how it would be in Jeb's interest to extend the project.

Gabe then talked about how Duke Farmer had felt obligated to be loyal to his VPs and how he had not had a chance to share his plan with him.

"Tell me why I shouldn't fire all of you and just hire someone else," Jeb asked angrily.

"Because I am the best engineer in the city and run the best department. My track record is phenomenal, and I would personally see to it that your project is my signature work. If you extend the timeline, you will win in more ways than one," Gabe responded.

There was a very long pause. And Gabe kept his eyes on Jeb.

Jeb turned his chair around and lit his pipe. He turned back and looked at Gabe.

"I admire you, young man. You must have been at the end of your rope to take this risk. All right, you got a deal. I'll pull the conversation to you tomorrow when we meet and you'll have the chance to sell it to Duke. He'll look at me, like he always does, and I'll nod. Twenty-six months you say? My people told me it would take thirty. I have known what you just told me all along. It's all business, young man, and be glad you don't know me that well. Yes, I already knew what you have just told me.

I am eager to work with you—I know you'll do fine. Stop by anytime."

"Thank you. Thank you very much," Gabe said finally.

He walked out and took a deep breath. He looked at the sky and felt alive. He knew he had just taken one of the most dangerous gambles of his life and won. He also knew that he would never do it again.

Would you have done what Gabe just did? Why or why not?

_____

_____

_____

Was Gabe justified in his final strategy?

_____

_____

_____

Was Gabe ethical in his final strategy?

_____

_____

_____

What would you tell Gabe if he told you what he had just done?

_____

_____

_____

Describe an experience where you were ethically challenged.

_____

_____

_____

How can you use your ethics to make important decisions?

_____

_____

_____

"The art of being wise is the art of knowing what to overlook."

—*William James*

Chapter Nine

Chapter Nine

WORK-LIFE BALANCE
NOVEMBER, 1999

A group of frogs were traveling through the woods, and two of them fell into a deep pit. All the other frogs gathered around the pit. When they saw how deep the pit was, they told the two frogs that they were as good as dead. The two frogs ignored the comments and tried to jump up out of the pit with all of their might. The other frogs kept telling them to stop, that they were as good as dead. Finally, one of the frogs took heed to what the other frogs were saying and gave up. He fell down and died. The other frog continued to jump as hard as he could. Once again, the crowd of frogs yelled at him to stop the pain and just die. He jumped even harder and finally made it out. When he got out, the other frogs said, "Did you not hear us?" The frog explained to them that he was deaf. He thought they were encouraging him the entire time.

This story teaches two lessons:

1. There is power of life and death in the tongue. An encouraging word to someone who is down can lift them up and help them make it through the day.

2. A destructive word to someone who is down can be what it takes to kill them. Be careful of what you say. Speak life to those who cross your path. The power of words...it is sometimes hard to understand that an encouraging word can go such a long way.

Author: Unknown
Source: Internet

The big story in America, and indeed the world, was the Y2K bug. Will the world shut down on the first day of the new millennium? How much cash should one take out of the bank? Survival lists comprising everything from batteries, generators, milk, bread, and peanut butter and jelly were circulating in every newspaper and magazine across the country. Pokemon was driving every parent crazy, and the Rams of St. Louis were winning.

Alex and Olivia were watching 'Who Wants to be a Millionaire?' when Olivia asked the age-old question: "So what would you do if you won a million dollars?"

What would you do if you won a million dollars?

    _____

    _____

    _____

Alex said he would put all of it into a college fund for the kids. He conceded that that was his constant financial challenge. He would pay off the house and get new cars if he had any money left over. Olivia concurred, and added that she would love to buy her dad a new car, too. She was tired of listening to him complain about his car always breaking down.

At about the same time in Chicago, Briana, too was watching a similar game show. But the prize money was two million dollars. And she began to think of what she might do with two million dollars.

*What would you do if you won **two** million dollars?*

_____

_____

_____

Briana was convinced she would open up her own dance studio and teach dancing seven days a week. She told herself she would market to the inner city children and charge a minimal fee. She began to think of incentives for girls that worked hard at dancing and were talented. She would give them all scholarships, she decided.

At about the same time in Charlotte, Gabe was getting ready to call Briana. They had become very close over the past few months and had begun to trust each other with their lives. Briana told Gabe about her two million spending spree, and Gabe suggested that he be allowed to invest in her studio. They opened their hearts to each other for about an hour and were looking forward to next month in Miami when they would all see each other again. They found it rather strange that almost a year had gone by. Gabe conceded that this had been the most eventful year in his life, and that he had grown more than he ever thought he needed to. He was thankful for Alex with whom he had become very close, and Iseus. They revered Iseus as a sage and wished everyone was lucky enough to have someone like him in their lives.

"Did you get the handouts for tomorrow's conference call?" Briana asked Gabe.

"Yes, but Iseus asked us not to look at them. So I didn't open his email. Did you?"

"Oh. All right, I confess. I did. When he asked us to block out two hours, I got curious. It was something about the Cycle of Life. It looked spiritual. Please don't tell them I peeked," Briana begged.

Gabe promised he would not and wished Briana a good night.

The next day at about 2PM, Gabe, Alex, Briana, and Iseus all called in on time. Iseus had asked that they all call from a place where they would not be interrupted. This would be one of their last sessions before Miami, Iseus said, and he needed to cover a good bit.

After the usual introductory comments about the weather, life at work, and the goings-on in the world, Iseus began the session.

"As future leaders, you will need to be very good at balancing your work and your life. But not in the traditional sense of work-life balance. When you think of balancing work and life—what do you consider your challenges to be?"

Answer this question for yourself.

_____

_____

_____

Gabe, Alex, and Briana brainstormed the following list:
- Career
- Individual time (e.g., working out or reading)
- Romantic time (spouse, significant other or dating)
- Family (immediate & extended)
- Community involvement
- Religious or spiritual time

Iseus then asked them to take these traditional challenges and think of a typical week in their lives.

"Out of 100%, list how much time in a week you spend on each one."

Answer this question below.

Career

Individual time   _____

                                  _____

Romantic time

_____

Family

_____

Community involvement

_____

Religious or spiritual time

_____

Total: *100%*

Below are the three responses:

Gabe

Career

_____70_____

Individual time

_____10_____

Romantic time

_____10_____

Family

_____0_____

Community involvement

_____0_____

Religious or spiritual time

_____10_____

Total: 100%

Briana

    Career

                                           55

    Individual time

                                           5

    Romantic time

                                         5

    Family

                                         5

    Community involvement

                                       20

    Religious or spiritual time

                                       10

  Total: 100%

Alex

    Career

                                       60

    Individual time

                                       2

    Romantic time

                                       5

    Family

                                       30

    Community involvement

                                       0

    Religious or spiritual time

                                       3

  Total: 100%

They debriefed the exercises. Since they had been communicating with each other frequently, the results did not surprise anyone.

Iseus then asked them to fill out their ideal week on the same worksheet.

Return to the previous page and write down your desired numbers next to your actual numbers. Remember, they must add up to 100. If there are gaps between the two, what would you be willing to change to get to the desired balance?

_____
_____
_____

What is keeping you from making these changes?

_____
_____
_____

If the above reasons are strong, what compromises, if any, are you willing to make?

_____
_____
_____

What could you change about your week to accommodate this compromise?

_____
_____
_____

Iseus took Gabe, Briana, and Alex through a similar set of questions. Gabe and Briana were able to think through how they could prioritize and organize their lives better. They made immediate changes to their schedule and promised to follow through on them.

Alex had little room to negotiate with himself. He had maximized his time and submitted that having a wife and three very young children forced him to be well organized. He simply had no choice. He acknowledged, however, how an activity like this might have helped him a few years ago, or could help him a few years from now. Iseus concurred and conceded that one size did not fit all.

"I'd like to share another model of work-life balance," Iseus offered. "It is called the Cycle of Life and does not require the type of shifting of schedules and priorities like the one we just did."

Iseus asked the group to pull out the Cycle of Life worksheet he had e-mailed them. He then asked them to put names of people in their immediate lives inside each of the boxes based on their age group. These names could not be mere acquaintances—they had to be good friends or people they interacted with on a regular basis.

Take a few minutes and fill out the Cycle of Life worksheet above. Real names of only the people you know well should be used. Write their names inside the boxes only. Do not be alarmed if you only know one or two names, or none at all for some boxes.

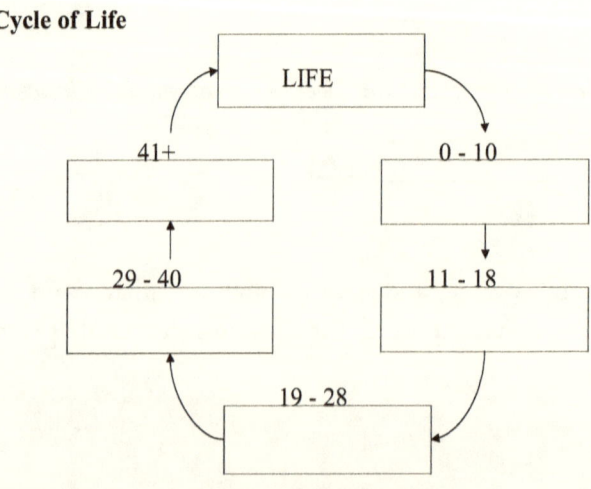

Cycle of Life

Iseus then instructed the three to look at the names in each of the boxes and for them to write down three descriptors on top of each box that best describes that age group. One way of coming up with a descriptor is to guess at how a particular age group views the world. For example, he suggested that 'Innocent' or 'Playful' might be good descriptors for the 0-10 age bracket.

Perform this instruction on your worksheet on the previous page.

He then asked the group to talk about the people in their boxes.

Alex had plenty of names in the 0-10 and 28-40 boxes (his age group) but only one or two in the rest of them. Gabe had no names in the 0-10 and 10-18 boxes. He had only a couple in the 18-28 and 40+ boxes and they were all from his workplace. Briana had the names of the children that she taught dance to in the 0-10 and 10-18 boxes. Her 28-40 box was filled with girlfriends, co-workers, Alex, Gabe, and Iseus. But with the exception of her parents, and a few old family friends, her 18-28 and 40+ boxes were not filled at all.

"I'm not sure I get the point," Alex asked politely.

"As managers, you are all at a crossroads in your personal and professional lives. **You must have a balance of the different views of life.** You cannot afford to forget where you came from—that will help you understand the people behind your box and you cannot afford to not know where you are going—that path you can get from the people in front of your box. The point, Alex, is wisdom. Who can tell me the difference between knowledge and wisdom?" Iseus asked.

What do you think is the difference between knowledge and wisdom?

_____

_____

_____

"I'll take a shot," Briana offered. "I think knowledge is like data, you know, just information. And wisdom is gained by using it correctly."

"I think I agree with that, Iseus," Gabe acknowledged.

Alex concurred.

"You're on the right track. I think of it terms of sharing. At the knowledge stage of processing our experiences, laying bricks, we understand what happened and why it happened but it is still in internal processing-mode. We own it. We are not ready to share it with others. We have not figured out how this knowledge could benefit others. Wisdom is harnessing that knowledge and realizing that the learning from the knowledge was not meant for just oneself. It is a humbling experience when you realize that you can take the knowledge achieved from your experiences (bricks of your house) and at the expense of your pain, decide you were going to figure out a way to let others benefit from it, and keep them from having to suffer through figuring it out. One makes a conscious decision to share these lessons with everyone—and create a closed and continuous learning system. This is how you contribute to the world.

The boxes in the Cycle of Life present you all with the opportunity to share—to teach and learn at the same time. If you want to be successful in life, and not just at work, you must fill in all the boxes with names and interact with them regularly. This is the Cycle of Life and work-life balance that will make you great people. **Great people quite naturally become great leaders**," Iseus concluded.

Gabe, Alex, and Briana were once again hijacked by Iseus' wisdom. They understood and could not believe how simple his philosophy was. The little voice in all their minds was telling them that he was right. What they had just heard would make them think differently about their lives. They were baffled at how centric their lives and perspectives truly were. And they had all thought of themselves as open minded.

Iseus asked them to pull out the second sheet he had emailed (see page 145) them and to think about the boxes that were not filled in. He then asked them to think of where they could go and what they could do to fill out all the boxes.

For all of the age groupings below that were not filled in your Cycle of Life, write down where you could go and what you could do to fill them in.

0-10

_____

_____

_____

11-18

_____

_____

_____

19-28

_____

_____

_____

29-40

_____

_____

_____

41+

_____

_____

_____

Iseus stayed on the line as they all filled out the second worksheet. Although some 15 minutes had gone by without a word being uttered, they all found great comfort in knowing that they were in this together.

Iseus instructed them to overlay their huts inside the Cycle of Life and to keep that image in their Day Timers to review frequently.

See above. Once you have completed this book, complete this holistic pictorial of who you are.

Cycle of Life

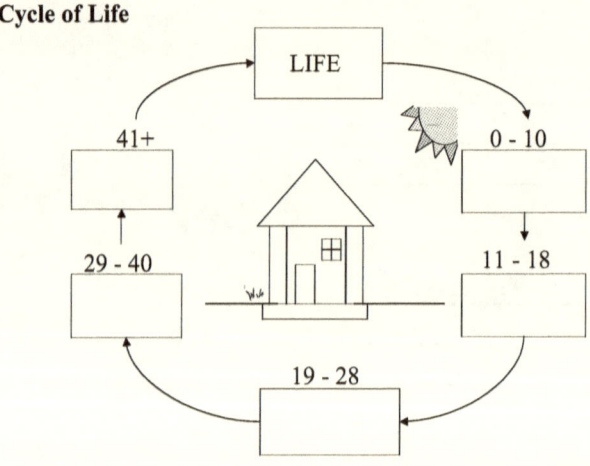

"How do you feel? What have you learned?" Iseus finally asked quietly.

Gabe and Briana both acknowledged how much work they still had to do in their lives. They promised to share their plans for the year 2000 when they met in Miami.

Alex was very pensive.

"You know, guys, in regard to wisdom and sharing, I do have a responsibility as a human being that goes beyond my family. I mean, my family comes first, but I know there are so many people at work that are either starting families or thinking about starting families and I could really help them. I'll talk to Gary about how to best do that. In fact, I put together a list here of the things I would recommend to young families while you all were still writing. Do you want to hear it?" Alex asked.

They all responded with a resounding "Yes."

Alex shared the following list with the group.

Recommendations for young families:
1. Dinner should be non-negotiable—all family members must be present
2. Let the kids make decisions—ask them what they want to eat or do
3. Share responsibility as much as possible—don't wait to be told what needs to be done around the house
4. Be active in the lives of other family members—be active in body and mind
5. Always talk and listen but not at the same time
6. No surprises—let each other know in advance if schedules/commitments change
7. Do one thing each day just for yourself
8. Don't forget your spouse is the person you married—keep the romance alive
9. Safely expose your children to the pains of this world—as adults, they will thank you for it
10. Expose the children to their extended family as much as possible—they will thank you for the friendships they make that will carry over into their adult lives

"Did you just come up with that? That's great. E-mail it to me," Briana requested.

"Just in the last five minutes and in random order. I can't wait to see all of you next month. Let's plan on dinner—just the four of us," Alex suggested.

They all agreed and were beginning to get genuinely excited about seeing each other.

"A measure of good health is the disposition to find good everywhere."

—Ralph Waldo Emerson

Chapter Ten

THE FUTURE OF MANAGERS
DECEMBER, 1999

People are often unreasonable,
Illogical, and self-centered,
Forgive them anyway.

If you are kind,
People may accuse you of selfish, ulterior motives;
Be kind anyway.

If you are successful,
You will win some false friends and some true enemies;
Succeed anyway.

If you are honest and frank,
People may cheat you;
Be honest and frank anyway.

What you spend years building,
Someone could destroy overnight;
Build anyway.

If you find serenity and happiness,
They may be jealous;
Be happy anyway.

The good you do today,
People will often forget tomorrow;
Do good anyway.

Give the world the best you have,
And it may never be enough;
Give the world the best you've got anyway.

You see, in the final analysis,
It is between you and you;

It never was between you and them anyway

Author: Unknown
Source: Internet

It was now only a couple of weeks away from the new millennium. A great deal of holiday shopping was going on. On-line shopping was the new craze, and millennium eve celebrations were being planned across the country. Office holiday parties were a nation-wide phenomena. A six-year-old Cuban boy, Elian Gonzalez, caught the nation's and world's attention as he survived sans his mother on a raft escaping Cuba. Florida State and Virginia Tech were going to play for the national football championship and Tiger Woods was winning everything. Two movies stood out: 'The Green Mile' and 'American Beauty'. Albert Einstein was voted Time's Person of the Century, and Amazon.com's Jeff Bezoz was the Person of the Year.

Gabe, Alex, and Briana all arrived on time in Miami for their three-day year-end session. They were delighted not just to see each other, but also to be in 80 degree weather in December. They had all dug out their summer wardrobes and were fully prepared to dress for the occasion.

Iseus had flown in a day earlier and was busy with the logistics of the entire session. On the eve of their first day, Gabe, Alex, and Briana met in the bar of the Doral Inn and Resort—home of the Blue Monster. Gabe and Alex had brought their golf clubs with them. Gabe and Briana met first and they gave each other the kind of hug one gives a good friend that hasn't been seen in years. Alex joined them later and received the same warm welcome.

They felt a little odd. They had talked to each other at least every two weeks in the past 10 months and shared intimate thoughts and feelings with each other. But they had not done that in person; looking at each other while they talked seemed strange. Nonetheless, they all had been looking forward to it for months now.

"So, what are you all doing for New Year's Eve?" Briana asked.

"I'm going to party downtown with some single guys from work. Nothing major, I guess," Gabe responded with a shrug.

"Home with the kids!" Alex yelled out. "Both Olivia's and my parents are coming over. We'll have all the TVs on and I hear most of the networks are going to show celebrations from around the globe starting with New Zealand and Australia. Of course, it helps that we all have Friday off to do that. It'll be fun. And you, Briana?"

"I'm not quite sure yet. My girlfriends are planning this limo party, and I think we'll be going to one of the hotels downtown. I wouldn't mind just staying home, you know?" she responded.

They talked until the bar closed at 2AM. They reminisced about the year and thanked each other for their support. Gabe told them about his job and shared the story of the stunt he pulled a few months earlier. Briana and Alex laughed and encouraged him to call them next time so he would not do anything so foolish again. The project was coming along quite well and he had become good friends with both Jeb Rose and Duke Farmer. In fact, he had an invitation to attend their New Year's celebration. None of the VPs were invited to that, Gabe noted.

He told them his divorce with Heather would be finalized in a few months and that he had only seen her once since the night they met briefly at The Pewter Rose restaurant. He had heard she would be getting married next summer and he admitted that he genuinely wished her well. He was glad he got to keep his home on the golf course. He also conceded that he had taken his work-life balance much more seriously and was 'good' to himself more. He had joined the YMCA and volunteered to coach a soccer team so he could fill in his 'boxes'. He said he was happy and at peace. He surprised Alex and Briana by telling them that he had just finalized his three-week trip to Africa. He would be leaving in February. He had hoped to have gone by now, but his new project delayed his plans.

Briana and Alex both commended Gabe for how far he had come over the past year. Gabe thanked them again.

"I can honestly say I could not have done it without you guys. I think about my loose bricks and my daily $100 of emotional energy everyday," he said.

Briana, too, shared how she was spending more time at Girl University. She rescheduled two afternoons a week to do that. She told Gabe and Alex about the WNTV and how she was consciously changing the right channel now. She also thought about perfect days. She was having more of them. She said talking to them and Iseus had become a part of her life and a part of her perfect day. Wednesdays were more perfect than other days. She was happy being single. She declared she would let fate decide her destiny but not her happiness. During Thanksgiving, she said she forced herself to imagine that it was her last Thanksgiving with her parents. She soaked up every minute and every moment of her five days with her parents and family. And yes, she said laughing, she did have her six-layered lasagna.

Alex said his day-to-day life on the outside had not changed that much, but he was more aware of himself, of what was important to him, and of what he could do with his limited time. He had indeed begun working with young families at work, and had become known as 'the family guy' in the office. He had just finished putting some structure around a support group. He was working in Atlanta and did not have to travel anymore.

Write down your key learnings thus far from reading this book

_____

_____

_____

_____

_____

_____

They all admitted that great conversation was the best part about friendship. And, like love or happiness, they could never have enough of it. Iseus told them in one of their conference calls that the number of topics yet to be discussed was so abundant that they were not capable of running out of conversation topics. They agreed and hoped to continue their friendship. They looked forward to seeing Iseus the next morning.

List some topics you would like to discuss with your best friends the next time you see them.

_____

_____

_____

The following day began with breakout sessions, unlike the first session in January. Iseus met Briana, Gabe, and Alex along with the other two groups of three. Gabe seemed surprised that the groups seemed to have bonded with Iseus as well as they had. He had thought they were particularly special to Iseus. His instinct told him they still were.

Iseus told the group that they would spend the morning with him and the afternoon with Darryl Bond. Darryl was going to talk about the future of managers and what he foresaw their challenges to be.

"But for the next few hours, we are going to do only one thing. All year long we have been learning different things about ourselves. I've worked with all of you and shared many different models with you. We need to put it all together. **Our approach was to get you to know yourself so you could have better relationships with yourselves.** Being great leaders is, and should be, a by-product of this healthy intrinsic relationship. **Only what you don't understand about yourselves will keep you from being happy and successful.** And that's why we've been doing all these strange exercises all year long.

We are going to learn to visualize. As future leaders, you will need to be visionaries. And I mean that literally. **You will have to be able to visualize the future in your minds and, more importantly, help your followers visualize your vision.** A picture is indeed worth a thousand words, but no one has a picture of tomorrow. These pictures only exist in one's mind and imagination, and if you can communicate that, then a leader you shall be indeed."

Iseus handed out two worksheets (see Figures 3 & 4) and gave the group the following instructions:

- There needs to be absolute silence during the course of the exercise
- Several questions will be asked; participants should respond in writing in the response boxes on Figure 1 (responses will not be shared)
- Responses should be as creative as possible
- Your goal should be to try and fill the brainstorming box with ideas; quantity is more important than quality here

You should adhere to the above instructions in order to proceed with this exercise.

Figure 3

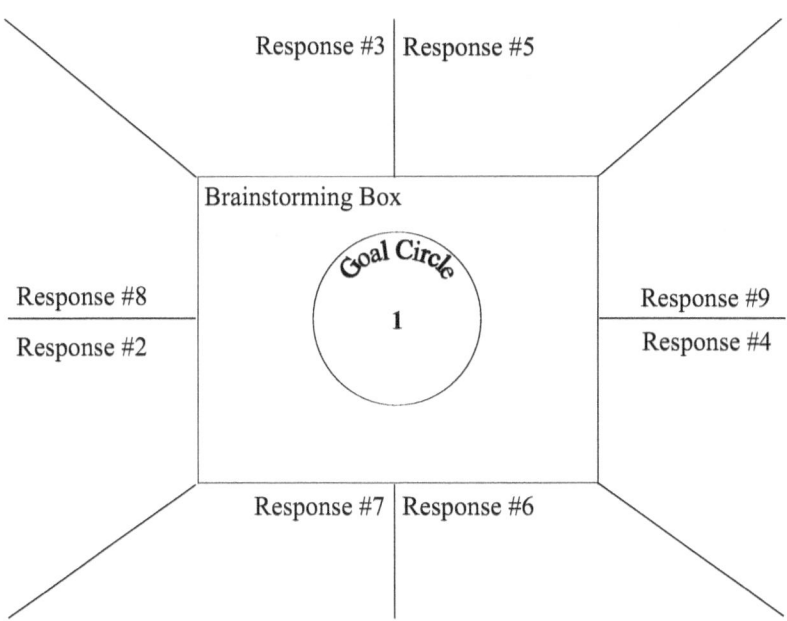

Iseus showed the group Figure 3 and explained what the goal circle, brainstorming box, and the response boxes were. He told the group to write down the responses to the questions he would ask in the corresponding numbered response boxes only. He was asking the questions specifically to stimulate their creative juices. Any ideas that came to the group during the questions should be immediately captured in the brainstorming box.

The group was ready and Iseus asked the following questions in the following sequence:

If you are ready to proceed, respond to each one of the questions below. Take a mandatory 60 seconds per question and after answering each question, take time to fill in your brainstorming box.

Question #1
In your goal circle, write down only one goal you have for the next year in a complete sentence. Carefully select the words for your sentence.

Question #2
In response box #2, write down two major barriers to achieving this goal.

Question #3
In response box #3, write down 3 items you need to achieve this goal. Begin to fill brainstorming box

Question #4
In response box #4, write down the first names of 3 people who can help you achieve this goal
Read the goal circle and add to the brainstorming box.

Question #5
In response box #5, write down two ways that these people can help you achieve your goal.

Question #6
In response box #6, write down the name of your best friend and next to his/her name, their favorite color—if you do not know their favorite color, make a guess.
Read the goal circle, response box #3 and add to the brainstorming box.

Question #7

In response box #7, write down the most creative thing you did in fifth grade, tenth grade, and in college.

Add to the brainstorming box.

Question #8

In response box #8, write down three strengths you were recently acknowledged for.

Read the goal circle, response box #5, and add to the brainstorming box.

Question #9

In response box #9, write down how your three strengths can help you achieve your goal.

Take five minutes to review your holistic hut, read your goal circle and response boxes #3, #5, #9, and complete filling in your brainstorming box.

Iseus then read the following facts to the group:

- Walt Disney was once fired for lack of creativity
- Michael Jordan, voted the greatest athlete of the century, was cut from his high school basketball team
- In 1875, the Director of the US Patents Office sent his resignation advising Congress to close his department—he said there was nothing left to invent
- Theodore S. Geisel's (Dr. Seuss) first children's book was rejected by 23 publishers; the 24th publisher sold six million copies
- Miracles happen everyday

He then instructed the group to take the brainstorming ideas and transfer them onto Figure 2. He further instructed them to insert those ideas into the three phases in a sequential and critical path manner. Phase 1 should have ideas that have to happen first, and Phase 3 were ideas of the final goal itself. Phase 2 are all the ideas that have to happen just prior to achieving the final goal. He gave them 15 minutes to do this.

Take a few minutes and transfer all your ideas to Figure 4 with the same instructions as above.

Figure 4

Phase 1	Phase 2	Phase 3
Ideas that must occur first	Ideas that must occur prior to total completion	Ideas of final image

Iseus asked the groups to look at the sequence they had created one last time. He then instructed them to free their hands, lean back in their chairs, close their eyes, and visually respond to the following questions. Iseus asked the questions very slowly.

As a reader, read all the questions below, *close your eyes* and formulate your image.

- Think of your goal.
- What do you see?
- Who is there with you?
- What are they wearing?
- What is the weather like outside?

- What colors do you see?
- What are you doing?
- What are you wearing?
- He paused for a few minutes.

Finally, he asked the group to open their eyes and complete Figure 4 with any additional ideas they had during their vision. That sheet would be their blueprint for their goal.

Complete your sequence worksheet.

Iseus asked the group how they felt. Many of them said they were able to visualize their goals with the process that Iseus had used. Some did not. To them, he insisted that the germane learning points were the questions they needed to ask themselves to coalesce their thoughts into a vision. They agreed.

"Actually, my image was very clear to me," Briana added. "I really took time to visualize what it was my goal looked like and it was like looking at a picture or a video. When you asked those questions with our eyes closed, I looked within the image and saw things I had not thought of. **I will use this process when I plan major goals, and I can use it with my teams and staff also.** But I do have one question, Iseus. Why did you ask us the question about our best friend and their favorite color?"

"**What hinders creativity are all the constraints of our surrounding environment and our frame of mind. These constraints steal from that emotional $100 worth of creative energy.** In being creative and brainstorming, you need to forget your next appointment or your next deadline. Asking a question like the friend's favorite color, which most people have not thought of, **forces you to search through a positive series of memories**, because it's your best friend, and find the answer. This adds to your $100 because that search takes you away from the constraints I just talked about," Iseus replied.

Gabe, Alex, and Briana were exhausted again, as they always seemed to be after a session with Iseus. It was lunchtime and Darryl was next. The three grabbed Iseus and asked him to join them for a farewell dinner. He obliged.

In the afternoon, Brian, Gabe, Alex, and Iseus all filed into the main ballroom overlooking one of the holes on the golf course. They saw many familiar faces from Atlanta and caught a glimpse of Darryl Bond heading towards the podium.

"Greetings everyone! Remember me? I'm the guy not related to James, James Bond," he said and received a few laughs.

"So, what have the last 10 months been like?"

This time he got a round of applause that lasted a good minute.

"Wow! I thought only we had fun," Gabe whispered into Briana's ear.

"This is good. Pay attention," she replied.

"So—what does the future hold for you?" Darryl asked.

"Promotion!" someone yelled from the crowd.

"Promotion is the easy part—the challenge is living up to your promotion. My mentor once told me that he never knew how good he was until he saw his competition. Folks, I disagreed with him then and I disagree with him today. I hope you've realized in the last 10 months that you are your competition. It is your loose bricks that need to be beaten-not the person sitting across the hall from you. It is those who use and refill their $100 of emotional energy that will lead a happy life. It is the people who have names in all the boxes of their Cycle of Life that will learn the most and be able to give the most. Those of you that treat your days as personal gifts and bow to your mortality will live lives that will continue to be relived after you die. Train yourselves to figure out what your Coefficient of Change is so you can effectively deal with Resistance Creep. Remember and acknowledge your Anchor Models.

Indeed, good people of the management persuasion, I come to tell you that your future is good only if you choose to embrace yourselves with humility, dignity, and self-respect. You came to us because you were talented—they send only the best of the best to our sessions. I hope you realized in the last 10 months that you're not the best. Neither I, nor anyone on my staff, is the best. I am still learning from children—I dare not assume the title of 'best' for myself.

The future of management is exciting. You have more opportunities to pursue than my generation ever did. They never had headhunters when I was your age.

The Internet and e-commerce is changing the way we do business. The talented and the entrepreneurial ones have golden opportunities. The Internet and e-commerce is giving you flexibility with your schedules and you can choose how many days you want to work and how long you'll work and how much of the rest of life you'll enjoy. The Internet and e-commerce is going to grow the niche players—do one or two things well and have everyone come to your own bedroom via the Internet to do business with you. Pretty cool stuff!

What types of people are you going to manage in this environment? Have you thought about that? Have you thought of what type of leadership it will take to manage the generation after yours? No? That's okay because we have. And the sad news is that you can throw away all the management books you read in MBA school. Tomorrow, your title will not give you leadership. Your flexibility with everything and everyone will. I can't tell you what skills to go acquire for tomorrow because I don't know what tomorrow will look like. But I do know that the human being is a master at survival and at teaching himself amazing things in amazing times in order to survive. Only the fittest will survive, Darwin said. The fittest will be those who know their souls, those who are kind and gentle spirits, those who view life as a journey of exploration and adventure, those who embrace change as casually as the change in the weather. What you will need for tomorrow is to know yourself better than you ever have before. Know your values and your ethics. Know your boundaries and limitations and remain loyal to the little voices in the back of your minds—only these voices speak during your internal stage performances.

Outsourcing is another trend, like the Internet and e-commerce, that will change the management of tomorrow. You have a skill, there's a demand, and you know the customer…let the customer pay you half what he's paying your employer which will still be twice what your employer is paying you. Man will always choose freedom over no freedom with a big title—Abraham Maslow taught us that 50 years ago.

What motivates you is a sense of progress and a sense of contribution—we said that already. Where can you find that? Fast-growing companies have plenty of room for thrill seekers wanting to add value. They are small enough to accommodate your passion. So the good money says more and more of you will leave your jobs so that you can grow faster.

But all is not lost for blue-chip America. Corporate America will always be here for the cautious—Dilbert has to make a living too. You must be extra careful though, not to look out your window because, as we've explained in the Emotional Theory of Relativity, you will see your friends that left your company and even younger people having more fun and making more money. You will be unhappy, not because of what you are doing but because of what you are not doing. You will wrestle with having responsibility but not authority. This group must find its sense of progress and contribution from outside sources, and those that do will be happy journeymen and women.

I don't know what path you must take and I presume, perhaps incorrectly, that you don't either. It's like deciding if you want to invest in the NASDAQ or the Dow Jones! That's okay. Look at your hut from time to time and change it from time to time—the world will get tired of looking at the same picture of you.

I hope we have gained from each other the intellectual moxie to figure it out. I wish you success in all you do for as long as you live, and pray I will hear about your happiness from time to time. Don't forget to share the short journey of life. Thank you."

This time, Darryl Bond received a resounding applause.

"That was quite a speech," Alex commented.

What is your future in your life and your company?

_____

_____

_____

What do you think management will look like in the next 5-10 years?

_____

_____

_____

How prepared are you for the changes that either you or Darryl Bond predicts?

_____

_____

_____

What excites you the most about your life, personal or professional, in the next five years?

_____

_____

_____

_____

_____

_____

That evening, Gabe, Alex, Briana, and Iseus took a cab to South Beach. They had all been looking forward to this for almost a year now.

They settled into the Cabana and chose a balcony table that overlooked the white beach. They could hear and feel the Atlantic breeze. It was a perfect evening.

"What shall we toast to?" Gabe asked.

"The future of us managers!" Briana yelled out.

"And to our souls," Gabe added.

"And to journeys!" Alex yelled with a smile.

"And to three of the best journey people I have ever traveled with," Iseus said calmly.

They toasted looking at each other. It was another strange feeling—the kind one has at the end of a long and gruesome journey. They knew they were better for it.

"So what now, Iseus?" Gabe asked.

"Now it's up to you all. The formal part is over. If you all want to continue to travel together, then do it. Teach and learn from each other. If not, that's okay too," Iseus replied.

They all agreed to continue as long as they could.

"How about you, Iseus. Will you join us?"

"I would be honored to," he replied.

They toasted again and recalled their pasts. They talked as though it were their last night together. They laughed and carried on until the restaurant closed at 4AM.

Upon arriving back at the Blue Monster, Alex and Iseus parted company first. Gabe walked Briana back to her room. As the night fell on the end of a year-long friendship, Gabe gently leaned over and kissed Briana passionately. She opened her eyes, looked at him calmly and smiled.

"Grab onto anything or anyone that makes you think..."

—Iseus

www.ingramcontent.com/pod-product-compliance
ming Source LLC
bersburg PA
W03094180526
63CB00002B/658